Cable Television and the First Amendment

Patrick Parsons
The Pennsylvania State University

Lexington Books
D. C. Heath and Company/Lexington, Massachusetts/Toronto

Library of Congress Cataloging-in-Publication Data

Parsons, Patrick.
  Cable television and the First Amendment.

  Includes index.
  1. Cable television—Law and legislation—United
States. 2. Freedom of speech—United States. I. Title.
KF2844.P37   1987   343.73'09946   86–45883
ISBN 0–669–14459–2 (alk. paper) 347.3039946

Published simultaneously in Canada
Printed in the United States of America
International Standard Book Number: 0–669–14459–2
Library of Congress Catalog Card Number: 86–45883

The paper used in this publication meets the minimum requirements of American National
Standard for Information Sciences—Permanence of Paper for Printed Library Materials, ANSI
Z39.48–1984. ∞™

87 88 89 90 8 7 6 5 4 3 2 1

Contents

Preface

Cablecasters began arguing for First Amendment rights in the 1960s. In the late 1970s and early 1980s it became something approaching an industry crusade. Thousands of pages of legal briefs, journal articles, and government and industry reports have been written on the topic. What I find most surprising, then, is not that a book entitled *Cable Television and the First Amendment* has been written, but that it has taken such a long time to come about. With the exception of the fine work, *Cable-Speech*, by George Shapiro, Philip Kurland, and James Mercurio, very little on the topic has been made available in book form to students of public policy or to the general public. Even in the works that do exist, the history and development of cable's First Amendment status has been much neglected. This book takes a close look at the evolution, in both regulatory and constitutional law, of cable's First Amendment position. It also penetrates and understands the underlying philosophical issues that comprise the debate. I hope, therefore, that it will help fill a few existing voids in the literature and promote the continued exploration of these problems.

Although the presentation is intended to be both thorough and detailed, it is not intended to be obscure. To the extent possible, I have avoided legal and social science jargon that might baffle and frustrate the lay reader. I hope, therefore, that the book will be accessible to all, and yet will retain material useful to the long-time student of communications policy.

In the six years since the inception of this book, many people have contributed ideas and support—first among them, my wife, Susan. Also providing continual encouragement and occasional funding were my parents, Judy and Mel. The good influence of my teachers, advisers, and colleagues at the University of Minnesota is, I hope, evident throughout the book; they include Irving Fang, Daniel Wackman, Chuck Bantz, the late Donald Martindale, and, most especially, Donald Gillmor. Other friends and colleagues who have aided in this effort include Ginny Parsons, Jack and Jean Strohm, Everette Dennis, Wayne Overbeck, Reed Parsell, and Mary Ann Manion. I thank you all.

1
Cable Television and the First Amendment

The viewer was frustrated. She adjusted the controls and checked the connections repeatedly, but could not get a clear picture. She had signed up to receive cable television at her home in Duarte, California several months before and had received the service, but still was trying to get a decent signal. She complained to the company and the city.[1]

It was not the only letter Duarte city officials received about the company, Acton CATV.[2] The complaints had been coming for years, and in January 1983 the city took legal action. Duarte withdrew the franchise that Acton had held to operate in the city, and began condemnation proceedings against the company's physical plant. Duarte was trying to get Acton out of town.[3]

The city's action raised a host of difficult legal questions. No one had ever tried to press condemnation proceedings against a cable company before. Did the city have the statutory or constitutional right to do so? What was the status of the company under state and federal law? The company certainly was providing a means of communication, of expression, for the community; were there any First Amendment considerations here?

The problem might never have arisen if the residents of Duarte had been able to switch to a competing cable company or simply get rid of the service entirely. But there was no other company in town, and some residents could not get a signal without the cable. Said one disappointed viewer, "If . . . we didn't have to subscribe, I don't think anyone would. We're captives."[4]

In 1986, a similar problem—consumer complaints about the service provided by the only cable system in the neighborhood—sparked another lawsuit, and raised similar questions. The New York Citizens' Committee on Cable TV claimed that the local cable system was trying to monopolize pay TV programming in lower Manhattan. The system was owned by Time, Inc., which also owned Home Box Office and Cinemax. It carried the Time pay TV services but did not carry the major competing services, Showtime and The Movie Channel, both owned by Viacom. The citizens' group claimed that Manhattan Cable was refusing to carry those and other competitors to maintain a pay TV monopoly.[5]

If the customers had been able to subscribe to another cable service, they very well might have. But there was no competitor. The city suggested that, under recently passed federal law, it was prevented from interfering in any of the company's programming decisions.[6]

Again, questions arose: Can a citizen or group of citizens legally force a cable company to carry programming it does not wish to carry? Could such a group, in a similar vein, force a local TV station to carry a new game show? Could it seek to require, through court action, that *The New York Times* carry a columnist that they admired, but the paper did not?

What if the question was not the absence of desired programming, but the presence of undesired programming. That question surely occurred to the citizens of Austin and Dallas when the local cable systems there began carrying a program called *The World As It Is*. The half-hour talk show was produced regularly by a former Grand Dragon of the Texas Ku Klux Klan. The message of the show was the message of the Klan: white supremacy.[7] Over the public access channels in Dallas, Austin, San Diego, California and other cities, the Klan was spreading its version of the gospel. City officials and civic leaders took a hands-off attitude, citing the fact that nobody seemed to be watching the programs and that organized protest would only draw attention to the Klan's activities.

But what if the programs became popular? What if they seemed to be leading to a resurgence of the racist organization and its cause? Would the temptation to censor grow? Would the group be denied access to the cable systems? Would the Klan have any rights under the Constitution to place its message before the people over the cable system? Would the cable company have any First Amendment right to block it?

Each of these situations raises an increasingly pressing question in modern American communications: that of the appropriate legal relationship between consumers, government, and cable television. These very real cable-citizen confrontations illustrate a myriad of growing and related concerns about cable TV access, rate regulation, licensing, service, ownership, and censorship. Most important, they are issues that are all linked by one overriding dilemma: What does the First Amendment have to say about cable TV? What are the First Amendment rights of cable operators, and what are the First Amendment rights of cable consumers?

As cable expands, as it enters more and more homes, as it becomes increasingly the channel through which Americans receive their nightly dose of news, entertainment, and information, this issue grows in importance. At the moment, it is still a problem for which there are more questions than answers. The constitutional boundaries that will shape the relationship between government, the public, and the cable industry are only beginning to take shape. Much remains ill-defined.

As such, the situation presents both serious problems and great opportunities. On the one hand, without clear guidance from the courts, statutory regulation of cable can, and has, varied with changing political fashions, over time and across jurisdictions. Confusion and contradiction over what is or isn't acceptable programming and behavior has often been the result. On the other hand, the opportunity now exists to establish a new set of guiding principles that will reconcile competing interests and assure the best possible use of the national cable network. But only a clear conceptual framework—a guiding principle of cable rights—will lead to a resolution of the problems and an exploitation of the opportunities.

This book examines the constitutional dilemma, analyzes its legal history, and suggests a means of formulating a new constitutional framework for cable, one that will provide a strong measure of protection against government interference in the operation of cable systems, and yet accommodate the legitimate First Amendment interests of the public in an open and diverse forum of cable communication.

The Constitutional Background

The first objective is to examine critically the development of cable's First Amendment status. The cable television industry's historic relationship with government might best be characterized as an unsatisfying roller coaster ride, a continually changing pattern of regulation and rationalization that has left many of the participants unhappy, most of them confused, and nearly all of them nervous, awaiting the next rise or dip in the political landscape. At its inception, cable television was virtually an unregulated, uncontrolled medium; the federal government found nothing it could legally control in early Community Antenna Television (CATV) and left the young industry alone. As cable grew, however, the concern of a strong potential competitor—the broadcast industry—grew as well, and along with it the concern of the Federal Communications Commission (FCC). In the early 1960s, the FCC assumed control of cable and throughout that decade heaped more and more rules on system operators. Constitutional concerns were not widely discussed.

The 1970s marked the beginning of a swing away from regulation, however, and most of the guidelines established during the decade of regulation were dropped by administrations moving toward a free market economy philosophy and general laissez-faire policies.

At the same time that the federal government was getting out of the business of regulating cable, cable operators were beginning to find a First Amendment voice. In the late 1970s and early 1980s, the industry began claiming a constitutional status equivalent to that of newspapers, magazines and books—a position often supported by the courts. For example, for more than a decade government—at either the local or the federal level—had compelled cable television systems to offer public access channels to allow citizens to present their ideas to the public. In the late 1970s a cable operator went to court to protest such regulation, claiming it violated his First Amendment rights.[8] For more than twenty years, the state has reserved the right to license or franchise cable systems to assure that they are being operated in the best interest of the community. In 1984 a cable company challenged such a law, again as a violation of the freedom of cable speech.[9] For nearly fifty years, the government has reserved the right to punish those who would distribute television programs that strayed beyond the limits of "decency." In 1982 a cable company went to court to argue that such laws violated fundamental First Amendment rights.[10]

Bringing these questions to the courts constituted the necessary first step in resolving them; it is the court system, and ultimately the United States Supreme Court, that is vested with the task of sorting out questions of constitutional law. But to date, this, in and of itself, has been insufficient to clarify the role of cable in a constitutional framework because the courts, in considering these questions, have provided precious few answers. The industry and others have, over the last fifteen or more years, repeatedly sought judicial guidance in the matter, but depending on the details of the case, the regulatory era in which the case was heard, and the particular jurisdiction in which the ruling was handed down, the courts have failed to speak with unanimity. Decisions of the court on cable's First Amendment status have varied widely in both detail and philosophy, often with direct conflict between and within jurisdictions.

Some courts, for example, have ruled that cable television has constitutional rights on a par with the print medium, which implies a strong shield against government regulation. Were this the case for all phases of cable operation, most of the rules now applied to cable might eventually be struck down. In contrast, other courts have found that the government has a legitimate right to regulate cable. Their rationale is that some special attribute of the medium sets it apart from print and opens the door to regulation. Among the attributes most often cited are cable's apparent status as a natural monopoly (the notion that only one system can operate in a given geographic area), the medium's use of public rights of way to lay cable, and cable's historic relationship with government. Each rationale has been attacked in and out of the courts; the question of cable's position as a natural monopoly has been hotly debated. It wasn't until 1985 that the Supreme Court, which must make the final determination, even agreed to hear a case involving a direct question of cable's constitutional standing.

This is not to somehow fault the courts. The issues are complex and the questions have changed over time. Still, the unfortunate result has been a continuing confusion by government, the industry, and the public about each party's First Amendment stake in the technology.

In the last few years a trend in judicial decision making has begun to emerge. This trend suggests an increasing willingness by the courts to accept the notion that cable television has strong First Amendment rights as an independent medium of communication. In fact, each year since 1980 seems to see another long-standing rule regarding cable TV struck down on constitutional grounds. Taken as a whole, the body of court decisions in the 1980s has reflected increasing constitutional protection for cable. Despite this, the universe of cable law, especially cable First Amendment law, is still very young. Much more needs to be resolved, and the question of the appropriate model of First Amendment rights for cable remains an open one.

Competing Models

What are the possibilities or alternatives in the debate? Throughout the historic conflict a variety of standard models of First Amendment rights have been posited. Most recently, as noted, a print model of First Amendment rights has been popular among industry spokesmen and proponents of general communications deregulation. Classically, however, the medium has been regulated pretty much along the lines of a broadcast model, and in the early years of cable regulation, the middle and late 1960s, there were numerous calls to govern cable as a sort of public utility, even a common carrier. Each of these forms of regulation has implied a very different relationship between cable and the state, and each has suggested a different set of constitutional rights for the medium.

Under the print model, cable would be free of much of the government control that exists today. It would enjoy the same protection under the First Amendment as newspapers, magazines, and books. In contrast, a broadcast model would permit government regulation similar to that known to radio and television stations. Whereas a print model would bar government control of the medium's content, a broadcast model would imply a reduced level of constitutional protection and permit the application of such rules as the Fairness Doctrine and Balanced Programming conventions. A public utility model conceivably would open the gates to even greater government involvement in the programming and service practices of the medium, again reducing the First Amendment barrier between government and speaker. Farther down the road toward government control, a common carrier model, a severe form of public utility, would have the effect of denying any First Amendment rights to the cable operator by denying the existence of cable as an autonomous First Amendment medium. The cable operator would become little more than a communications facilitator or broker.

An alternative approach to the question of the appropriate model of cable rights reaches beyond the cable question to consider the nature of First Amendment protection as it is differentially applied to the various media. The approach directly attacks the assumption that there ought to be different levels or standards of constitutional rights for print as opposed to broadcast or cable media. It points out that, as technology advances and starts to combine various media forms, the technological characteristics that distinguish communications systems begin to blur. The melding of communications technologies, therefore, ought to lead to a unification or integration of First Amendment theories. This integrated model suggests that a single, unifying framework of First Amendment rights be applied to all media regardless of their current technical structure or capacity.[11]

Unfortunately, the integrated model butts directly into the reality of Supreme Court precedent. The high court historically has rejected the notion that a given standard of First Amendment rights can be applied uniformly to all media. Each form of communication must be considered in terms of its own unique characteristics, according to the Court.[12] As early as 1949, Justice Felix Frankfurter addressed the issue, stating:

> It is argued that the Constitution protects freedom of speech: Freedom of speech means the right to communicate, whatever the physical means for doing so; sound trucks are one form of communication; ergo that form is entitled to the same protection as any other means of communication, whether by tongue or pen. Such sterile argumentation treats society as though it consisted of bloodless categories. The various forms of modern so-called "mass communication" raise issues that were not implied in the means of communication known or contemplated by Franklin and Jefferson and Madison. Movies have created problems not presented by the circulation of books, pamphlets or newspapers, and so the movies have been constitutionally regulated. Broadcasting in turn has produced its brood of complicated problems hardly to be solved by an easy formula about the preferred position of free speech.[13]

Cable, like other new technologies, has raised its special and unique constitutional quandries. Because of this strong tradition of Supreme Court precedent, this study begins with the assumption that the Court will continue to seek special and individually tailored solutions to the difficult social, economic, and, finally, legal questions that are created by each new media form.

Ultimately, then, this book examines the usefulness of each of the major models suggested above in addressing the constitutional issues raised by the evolution of cable television. The power and flexibility of the models, their intrinsic ability to satisfy a variety of competing and often antagonist First

Amendment claims, will be the focus of much of the discussion, for, in fact, the nature of the whirlpool of competing First Amendment interests lies at the center of cable's constitutional dilemma.

The Theoretical Debate

The real heart of the cable controversy is the tug-of-war between the First Amendment claims of cable operators and the First Amendment claims of society. In theory, the constitutional guarantee of freedom of expression should serve to benefit both the individual and the collective. It should provide the legal context for the expression of an individual's deeply held beliefs and opinions. It also should protect the forum by which those ideas are communicated to the public, and assure that the society has uninterrupted access to those ideas. It is common for the courts to cite both rationales when striking down government intrusion into the area of free speech. But there are situations in which these constitutional goals work against, rather than with, each other; the question of cable television's constitutional status is one such situation. Should the First Amendment be a shield to protect cable operators from state interference in the operation of their communication systems? Or should it be a sword to cut through barriers restricting the flow of cable-delivered information to the people? Perhaps, as is often the case, the best answer lies somewhere in the middle. So the question becomes: Which, if any, of the traditional models of cable regulation is best suited to strike the balance?

This book argues that none of the standard models are satisfactory answers to the problem. Each fails in some way to provide for the legitimate claims exercised by the important actors. To adequately balance the competing interests requires a new approach to both the theory and application of the First Amendment in this context. Such an approach will be outlined and defended in the second part of this book. The product of this new perspective is a model that would free cable operators from most of the government constraints on content, structure, and behavior to which they have historically been subjected, and so provide a stronger measure of constitutional protection for the individual operator. At the same time, the model locates in the First Amendment a rationale for limited access to monopoly cable systems that ensures the collective an uninhibited marketplace of cable expression. This access mechanism distinguishes itself from previous similar proposals by finding its source in the Constitution rather than in legislative or regulatory policy, and by applying differentially across the major forms of media (and, importantly, applying not at all to the print media). While not a perfect solution, the argument will be presented that it is a better balance than can be struck in alternative models.

The Plan of the Book

Before launching into this broad analysis of constitutional models, it is necessary to understand the growth and development of cable regulation as it
relates to the issue of freedom of expression. Therefore, the question of the
evolution of cable's constitutional status will be considered at the outset.

The concern about cable's First Amendment role is not a new one. The
courts, the Congress, and the Federal Communications Commission have
grappled on and off with the problem for more than twenty years, and, over
the course of decision making, we can see a definite evolution in the perception of cable's constitutional standing. The first few chapters consider the
rise of cable's First Amendment status and suggest that regulators have responded to, and have made policy decisions based upon, a given, current
definition of the situation, and that the temporal, operative definition with
respect to cable has progressed through several clearly defined phases or
definitional paradigms. That is, different regulatory actors can be shown to
have held different definitions of the medium throughout its development.
Whether or not these definitions truly reflected the characteristics of the
medium, they were, nonetheless, the basis upon which regulation proceeded.
While the medium developed gradually in both technical and economic dimensions, dramatic changes in how it was defined by policy makers often
came about as the result of social forces outside the medium itself. The
substantive changes in cable regulation and the nature and types of First
Amendment questions that arose in those policy proceedings can be viewed
from this perspective, thereby helping illuminate the reasons for change and
the outcomes of policy.

The book, then, is divided into ten chapters. Chapter 2 supplies a historical context by presenting a broad overview of the technical, economic,
and regulatory development of the cable television industry. Chapter 3 examines the role of the First Amendment in the history of policymaking by
the FCC and Congress. It focuses on the role of definitional paradigm change,
how the change in the definition of cable TV affected both regulatory and
constitutional deliberations. Chapter 4 considers at length the question of
how the courts have viewed cable's First Amendment role. It examines changes
in court thinking and the problems of inconsistency in judicial decisions.
Chapter 5 opens the second section of the book with a discussion of the
goals of the First Amendment and the problems encountered when those
goals collide. It presents a general theory of First Amendment rights with
which to measure specific models of cable TV protection. The broadcast
model of cable rights is critiqued in chapter 6, and the print model in chapter
7. Chapter 8 briefly considers the applicability of a public forum model for
the protection of cable expression, and chapter 9 looks closely at a general
public utilities model and a more specific common carrier model of cable

rights. The concluding chapter proposes an equitable protection model, outlining both its constitutional justification and the likely impact of its adoption on the industry.

Summary

Cable television is increasingly becoming a part of our media lives. It brings us entertainment, sports, news—ideas. Yet, we have no clear notion of the constitutional rights of those who own, program, and view the medium. In the past, the First Amendment rights of the system owner and operator were sacrificed for the benefit of the community. Now the pendulum is swinging back, and soon the community may have very little say in what the local cable system distributes or refuses to distribute. This book attempts to clarify the issues, delineate the stakes in the game, and propose a method by which the many competing interests can find a First Amendment compromise that protects the goals of freedom of expression in their many different and important forms.

Notes

1. *See*, "Cable Subscriber Makes Federal Case Out of It," *Los Angeles Times*, 30 August 1983, at pt. 6, p. 8.

2. *Id.*

3. The action eventually was settled in favor of the city without much attention given to constitutional questions by the court. *Acton CATV, Inc. v. Duarte*, No. CV 83-1018 (Feb. 28, 1984).

4. *Supra* note 1.

5. "Manhattan Cable Sued Over Access," *New York Times*, 30 January 1986, at pt. C, p. 20.

6. *Id.*

7. J. Schwartz, "Austin Gets an Eyeful," *Channels of Communication*, March/April 1985, at 44.

8. *United States v. Midwest Video Corp.*, 440 U.S. 689 (1979).

9. *Preferred Communications, Inc. v. Los Angeles*, 754 F.2d 1396 (9th Cir. 1985).

10. *Home Box Office v. Wilkinson*, 531 F. Supp. 987 (D. Utah, 1982).

11. *See e.g.*, A. Branscomb, *The First Amendment as a Sword of a Shield: An Integrated Look at Regulation of Multi-Media Ownership*. (P-5418) (Santa Monica, CA: The Rand Corp., 1975).

12. *Joseph Burstyn v. Wilson*, 343 U.S. 495, 503 (1952); *Kovacs v. Cooper*, 336 U.S. 77 (1949); *Red Lion Broadcasting v. F.C.C.*, 395 U.S. 367, 386 (1969).

13. 336 U.S. at 96.

2
The Evolution of the Industry

A careful consideration of the First Amendment rights of cable-delivered expression cannot be adequately undertaken without repeated reference to the historic development of the cable television industry. This chapter traces in broad strokes the technological, economic, and political forces that shaped the industry's structure and, more importantly, shaped the popular definitions of cable TV. An appreciation of the changing concept of cable television and the evolving philosophy of its potential in society is key to a full understanding of the relationship between the medium and the First Amendment. These first pages, then, provide a historic context for subsequent detailed discussions of the protection that has been and ought to be extended to cable speech.

A Systems Model

While the driving force behind the development of the cable industry has been economic and the enabling force technological, more often than not the controlling force has been regulatory. Government in its various forms has acted alternatively to restrict and foster the forces of marketplace and workshop, determining to a large extent when and where cable will prosper. Therefore, the analytic focus may most profitably be turned here to the regulatory sphere, pulling in the economic and technical elements as the need arises. Krasnow, Longley and Terry provide a general systems approach for the analysis of government policy toward broadcasting that is well suited to this task.[1] The model they've outlined accommodates the roles of the FCC, the industry, Congress, the public, special interest groups, and the White House. It proposes an open system of telecommunication regulation which tends to be simultaneously proactive and reactive; it responds to stimuli from outside system boundaries while developing policy that sets the context for new stimuli. It is a cyclical process of change with a network of feedback channels. The system, therefore, also can be characterized as morphogenic in that the number and types of elements that represent system components are found to change gradually over time. This evolution in the system itself, of course, accounts for much of the change in policy.

These qualities of the model—a twin reactive and proactive attitude plus an evolutionary nature—make the general systems approach particularly powerful in explaining the development of cable television regulation, for the story of cable is not so much one of carefully planned growth as it is of conflict and compromise among many different and antagonistic players.

The Early Years

The first cable television station is reported to have been built in Astoria, Oregon in 1949. It was noncommercial.[2] The first commercial system began in Lansford, Pennsylvania, where the valleys of that state quickly became the spawning ground for what was then called Community Antenna Television (CATV).[3] The reasons for cable's successful development there are unambiguous. Cable was the joint product of technologically created consumer need and entrepreneurial foresight. The need arose from the inability of people in the Pennsylvania valley towns to receive clear television signals. Television was new at that time so only the larger towns had stations, and the mountains prevented a clear signal from reaching the outlying areas. The first cable operations often were built by TV dealers and servicemen who hoped to spur sales of television sets by providing potential customers with a television signal.[4] In addition to what they hoped would be increased sales of sets, the cable operators made money by charging for the installation of the cable and by levying a monthly service fee. The installation charge was about $100; the monthly fee ran from $3 to $7, for which customers received a clear signal from three or four stations.[5]

The fruit of this new system was sweet for all who took part in the harvest. The public received crisp television signals, the small businessman received a fair profit, and the television station owner received a larger audience, potentially justifying an increase in the price of airtime he sold to advertisers.[6] Consequently, during this early period—from about 1950 to 1955—there was little pressure for the regulation of cable. Local government was involved only to the extent that permission was required to lay cable over public property.[7] The FCC was aware of the existence of CATV[8] but some suggested that it was viewed as a monetary aberration in the national broadcasting system.[9] In fact, congressional testimony supports the claim that the feeling at the commission was that, as VHF and UHF television stations multiplied in the smaller towns and cities, the need for cable television would dissipate and the technology would die on the vine.[10]

From the viewpoint of systems theory, the lack of federal intervention at this point in cable's history is not surprising. Little or no stress was placed on the regulatory system, and therefore little or no action was required. Further, any pressure for action would have been tempered or dispersed through the predictive nature of the system, which forecast an eventual deterioration of the cable industry.[11] But cable was not an aberration; it grew tremendously. Total subscribers mushroomed from 14,000 in 1952 to 150,000 in 1955. The total number of systems grew from 70 to 400 in the same period.[12]

Most of these systems were small, serving communities that lacked nearby TV stations, or where reception of nearby stations was weak. But as the industry grew, it moved into towns with existing television outlets. For the broadcast station owners, the construction of a cable system in their market generally meant only one thing, unwanted competition. The CATV operation could offer viewers an alternative to what was often a monopoly TV signal by importing, via microwave, television stations from distant towns. Moreover, such importation occasionally duplicated the programming aired by the local station, presenting local broadcasters with the potential loss of a lucrative monopoly market.

This economic confrontation provided the first significant stimulus to the regulatory system. Cable was moving from a beneficial, or at least benign, adjunct to television toward a competitive threat which, in turn, prompted broadcasters to begin considering legal protection of their financial interests. The regulatory system to which those concerned broadcasters appealed for relief was, according to Krasnow and Longley, relatively uncomplicated at the time, being comprised of only three important actors:

> Congress, the FCC and the (broadcast) industry itself. These were the three focal points of a closely knit triangle of pressure, cooperation, and shifting alliances. The lines of influence were clear, and the industry knew how to work for what it wanted.[13]

A change in the broadcast industry's definition of the situation, then, prompted a behavioral response manifested procedurally in an appeal to the regulatory system. The first formal step in the process was a request in 1956 by a coalition of thirteen broadcasters from the western states to have the FCC take control of cable television.[14] In this case, *Frontier Broadcasting v. Collier,* the broadcasters claimed a severe threat to their economic viability if cable was permitted to grow unrestrained. The commission denied their request on the grounds that evidence of the claimed damage was unconvincing and that the FCC's legal authority in the area was unclear.[15]

Looking closely at the records of the time, startling differences appear in the perception of cable between the FCC and broadcasters. The commission remained a captive of the older, more passive definition of cable as an economically nonthreatening TV service,[16] while the broadcasters had sub-stantially modified their view.

With the FCC declining to act, broadcasters went to the other major participant in the regulatory process: Congress. Under broadcaster lobbying, the Senate Commerce Committee held hearings in 1958 on the impact of cable on local broadcasters.[17] While no legislation resulted, there was some congressional criticism of the manner in which the FCC had handled cable affairs,[18] and pressure to have the FCC reconsider the cable problem in-creased.[19] With such prodding, the commission took another look at the situation in 1959, but this second investigation was to prove even less sat-isfying to broadcasters. On April 14 of that year the commission formally declared that under the Communications Act of 1934—its charter legisla-tion—it had no authority to regulate CATV.[20] Under the Communications Act, the commission could regulate broadcasting and common carrier sys-tems, but cable, said the commission, was neither. It was up to Congress, said the FCC, to grant such oversight.

Obligingly, the Senate Commerce Committee met to consider action.[21] This time the hearings culminated in a bill, introduced by Senator John Pastore, that would have given the FCC explicit authority to regulate cable.[22] The bill narrowly missed passage, but observers suggested that the intensity of industry and congressional feeling on the issue had a decisive impact on the commission and led eventually to an FCC decision to reverse its 1959 ruling and finally take control of cable.[23] That action came in 1965 and could more accurately be described as a circumvention than a reversal.

The process began with a series of 1958 FCC hearings on CATV, when the National Association of Broadcasters (NAB) argued that the FCC did indeed have authority to regulate cable through its jurisdiction over micro-wave communication.[24] The commission ignored the argument at the time, but in 1961 a cable operator's application for a microwave license was chal-lenged by a local broadcaster and the idea resurfaced.[25] The company, Carter Mountain Transmission Corporation, sought permission to import distant signals using microwave. Perhaps as a result of broadcast industry and congressional pressure, the commission was more eager than it had been in 1958 to find a means of asserting jurisdiction. It reached back to the NAB argument of three years before and determined it had the power to deny a microwave license to a cable operator. If Carter Mountain or any other cable operator wanted a microwave license, said the commission, it would have to agree not to import distant TV signals that duplicated local programming (nonduplication rules) and guarantee carriage of local signals (carriage rules). The restrictions were imposed on the basis of potential economic harm to the local broadcasters and subsequent deterioration of community TV service.[26]

The underlying philosophy expressed by the FCC was that the public interest was best served by local television stations, and any threat to those stations represented a threat to the public service that the commission was sworn to protect. As FCC Chairman Rosel Hyde later told Congress, the intent was "to integrate the CATV operation into the national television structure in a manner which [did] not undermine the television broadcast service."[27] Other observers suggested that the commission simply was responding to broadcast industry pressure, and early regulation represented "an apparent hostility toward letting cable grow as its own ingenuity and consumer acceptance may have dictated."[28]

Whatever the rationale for the Carter Mountain decision within the framework of the systems model, the 1962 ruling represented the first movement by the FCC toward congruence with Congress and the broadcast industry over the new definition of cable as a more active element in the communications mix. It was the first formal set of controls placed on the medium.

Regulation

Lengthy hearings on cable followed Carter Mountain with the FCC concluding in 1965 that it would serve the interests of efficiency to issue blanket guidelines for CATV rather than deciding each case as it came before the commission.[29] But, in keeping with the justification for jurisdiction in Carter Mountain, the guidelines, imposing carriage and nonduplication restrictions, applied only to those cable systems with microwave feeds.[30]

Meanwhile, cable was threatening to break out of its role as a service to smaller communities and enter the larger, metropolitan areas.[31] The giants of the broadcasting industry with most of their holdings in these larger markets previously had been able to sit complacently and watch the western and small-town broadcasters fight cable. But the developing CATV industry now posed a threat, and major industry groups such as NAB exerted new pressure on the FCC for relief.[32] According to some observers,[33] such pressure was at least one factor in the FCC's 1966 decision to assert jurisdiction over all CATV operations and impose stringent controls to prevent cable's penetration of the larger markets.[34] Such control went beyond previous decisions by applying even to cable operations that did not use microwave. However, the expansion of its control forced the commission to abandon the thin pretense that it could regulate only on the basis of microwave use. The new rationale for regulation was purely the economic impact that cable might have on broadcasting.[35]

As a part of this decision, the 1966 Second Report and Order, the FCC imposed rules preventing CATV systems from importing signals into the top 100 markets. The commission explained these rules as a protection for the struggling UHF service which it felt had the best chance in the larger markets.[36] Critics, however, claimed that UHF would have gained little from the ban since it had more formidable barriers to its development than CATV, and that the real beneficiaries of the rule making were the larger, established VHF stations in the top markets.[37] To the extent that this accusation might have been accurate, it represented a shift by the FCC from a concern with the protection of TV stations in smaller markets to a concern about the threat to the major market stations in the broadcast system.

The impact of the 1966 rule making on cable operators was to effectively shut them out of the top 100 markets, markets that represented eighty-nine percent of all the television homes in the country.[38] Without program material from its most readily available source, out-of-town TV stations, the cable industry had little to offer potential customers in the larger cities, and without a product the industry could not expect to prosper.[39] Therefore, the structure of the regulatory system and the interests and positions of the major participants made it appear, as of the mid-1960s, that cable's future was destined to be one of rural, ancillary television service.

New Life

Had the tripartite model of decision making which dominated the broadcasting arena remained stable, this picture might not have radically changed. But the social forces of the mid- and late 1960s rearranged many institutions, including those related to broadcast regulation. Krasnow and Longley elaborate:

> [T]his balance of forces which prevailed for so long [was] altered . . . by the increased involvement of three participants in broadcast regulatory policy making: the public in the form of citizen's groups; the White House, by means of special advisory bodies and government bureaus; and the courts, in the form judicial opinions prescribing and precluding F.C.C. policy initiatives. Together, the development of these three activist participants in broadcasting regulation . . . modified the Commission's role from one of making peace with Congress and a dominant industry, to one of attempting to placate several often antagonistic interests.[40]

For the cable industry, the new involvement of citizens' groups, particularly private and public research organizations, was especially important at this time. The spell of new technology and the promise of a new means to cope with old social ills was beginning to take hold in the imaginations of social philosophers and planners around the country. This excitement translated into political pressure to promote cable growth.

A variety of influential governmental and nongovernmental agencies released reports on the possibilities of cable television in the mid- and late 1960s and early 1970s.[41] One of the first, New York City, issued a lengthy study in 1968 praising the technology and urging development of a citywide system, suggesting that cable offered a solution to a variety of problems present in the modern urban environment.[42]

Similar reports, several of them direct responses to the FCC's call for comments on the future of cable regulation, were released in 1971.[43] Some were highly successful in rallying the public to the cause of cable. Ralph Lee Smith's *The Wired Nation* was a prominent example.[44] This magazine article turned book was one of the first major publications to stir the imagination of influential segments of the public.

The expanding role of the White House in the regulatory mix also may have affected cable development. In 1968, The President's Task Force on Communication Policy released a report calling for an enlarged role for cable in the national communications complex, providing another strong voice in the call for continued cable development.[45]

To this new regulatory pattern, a fourth participant was added, a still small but growing cable industry. While no match for the behemoth broadcasting lobby, this new actor was beginning to find a voice in the diversifying regulatory process.

Finally, there were indications that the FCC itself was changing and was becoming more receptive to the increasing pressures to reexamine cable's place in the mass communication system. According to public policy analysts Besen and Crandall:

> The opportunity for cable to break these shackles [of restrictive regulation] occurred when Dean Burch replaced Rosel Hyde as Chairman of the F.C.C., several other commissioners' terms expired, and the Office of Telecommunications Policy was established under Clay Whitehead.[46]

Both Burch and Whitehead were seen as sympathetic to cable television and committed to promoting the interests of new technology.[47] Their emphasis seemed to be on breaking down regulatory barriers to cable's entry into major markets. In short, the regulatory structure was rapidly changing. A new model was being molded, and young forces within it were exerting pressure for a modification, or at least a review, of restrictive cable regulations.

At the same time, cable was slowly growing, and other actors in the system began reevaluating their positions, reexamining the nature of their interests in the system. Cable historian M.H. Seiden suggests, for example, that increasing broadcast ownership of cable systems softened broadcasters' opposition to cable growth.[48]

Further, the cable industry appeared more willing to compromise on issues of controversy, an attitude that was most important in the hard-fought issue of copyright.[49] Broadcasters had long complained that cable operators were stealing their TV signals, that the process of cable retransmission of TV constituted a violation of the broadcaster's copyright. The courts ruled against the broadcast industry on this issue,[50] but the industry continued to lobby Congress and the FCC for copyright protection. Indications that the cable owners were open to proposals for accepting a form of copyright liability helped in reducing the antagonism of some broadcasters.

Another issue of contention was the number of TV signals a cable operator could import into any given market. As has been suggested, the FCC, in early rule making, had placed great emphasis on the economic harm such importation might do to local broadcasters, but studies conducted in the late 1960s and early 1970s provided evidence that the FCC and broadcaster fears were overstated.[51] These findings, according to Besen and Crandall, went far to ameliorate the commission's concerns about the impact of cable on broadcasting.[52]

In short, changes in the regulatory structure and the posture of some actors in the system both preceded and accompanied the formal regulatory process by which cable rules were reconsidered and modified in the late 1960s and early 1970s.

The first step in the formal process of change began with the FCC's Notice of Proposed Rulemaking in 1968.[53] A long and complicated struggle followed among all of the above mentioned parties, resulting in a series of interim and proposed rules and finally culminating in a 1972 compromise that served as the foundation of cable regulation through the 1970s.[54] The highlights of the process are summarized below:

1969

The FCC issued rules requiring cable systems of specified size to originate their own programming.[55]

1970

The FCC issued a series of proposed rules affecting signal importation and proposing a plan whereby cable television would underwrite public television.[56] The proposals were dropped following opposition from broadcasters. The FCC began formulating new rules. Senator Pastore, Chairman of the Senate Communications Subcommittee, and Representative Torbert MacDonald, Chairman of the House Communications Subcommittee, notified the FCC that no new cable rules should be promulgated without prior review by their subcommittees.

1971

FCC Chairman Dean Burch sent a letter of intent to Congress outlining the commission's proposals for new rule making. The proposed rules were attacked by the broadcast industry, which took its case to the White House. The President assigned Clay Whitehead, director of the Office of Telecommunications Policy (OTP), to act as arbitrator between the disputing interests.

1972

The FCC issued new rules concerning the regulation of cable television. The regulatory package was based on the so-called Whitehead compromise, which the OTP head had forged.[57]

Under the provisions of the 1972 rules, cable systems were granted the right to import distant signals into the major markets, but severe limitations were placed on the number and types of signals that could be brought in. The systems were required to carry signals from the three networks that were to originate from the nearest affiliate to the given system, part of the so-called anti-leapfrogging rules.[58] If signals from independent television stations came from one of the top twenty-five markets, they had to come from one of the two largest markets closest to the system's market.[59]

The number of signals the system could import depended upon the size of its market. Systems in the top fifty markets could carry the signals of three network and three independent stations. Systems in markets 51 through 100 could import three network signals and two independents. Systems in the markets below 100 could carry the three network signals but only one independent.[60]

Broadcasters were protected by extensive nonduplication guidelines. Cable operators could not show a program from the imported stations if a local broadcaster owned exclusive rights to that program in that market. And even if no such exclusivity agreement existed, the retransmission of certain syndicated programs by cable operators was prohibited in a complicated time-based formula.

The new rules also required cable operators to provide free access channels for use by the public at large, local government, and local educational institutions. Various technical standards also were imposed on the cable systems.[61] In general, greater restrictions were placed on cable systems operating in the larger markets.

The new rules represented a swing away from the more stringent regulations of the past that had placed a lid on cable growth in the larger cities, but many questioned whether the apparent easing of restrictions provided any real relief for the stifled cable industry. There was much concern that the new rules did not go far enough in freeing cable and, therefore, left the industry in no better shape than before the lengthy hearings and rule making. Cable industry analyst Anne Branscomb observed at the time that the rules were so stringent that cable might prosper in only 17 of the top 100 markets.[62]

Ralph Smith was more pointed in his comments. He declared that:

> The Federal government remains firmly committed to preventing cable from overcoming the inequalities in the U.S. commercial system of broadcasting. . . . The rules do not prohibit the building of cable systems in the nation's top 50 markets, but they are designed to retard it, and there's little doubt that they will succeed in doing so.[63]

The ability of the cable industry, therefore, to break into the major markets in the United States in a meaningful way was not significantly advanced by the new rules. The cable industry remained relegated to a minor and financially impotent role in the broader communications system of the United States.

So, as cable moved into the mid-1970s, regulatory constraints continued to hamper its growth. The situation was exacerbated by a generally poor economic climate and a growing investor cynicism fostered by failed industry promises. The sheer cost of building a cable system, for example, skyrocketed. In the 1960s, the cost of laying one mile of cable, according to Branscomb, averaged around $3,500.[64]

This price had doubled by 1973, and some cities were requiring that the cable be run underground instead of strung on poles. The cost of constructing an underground system could run anywhere from $9,000 to $50,000 a mile. In addition, money with which to finance construction was becoming more difficult and costly to obtain. Debt service increased from a relatively tolerable six percent in the late 1960s to eleven percent in 1973, and a softening economy made it more difficult for the young and untested cable industry to secure financial support even when it was affordable.[65] Compounding this problem, according to Branscomb, was a growing skepticism by lenders who saw the much touted promise of cable failing to materialize. Branscomb placed some of the blame on the industry itself, which she claimed oversold its potential in the late 1960s in order to make its stock more attractive to potential investors.[66]

In summary, the restrictions on signal importation, pay cable, and program duplication—along with a shaky economic foundation—made cable television in the early 1970s appear to be a communications technology whose time had not yet come.

The Latter 1970s

While cable plodded along successfully in the smaller markets through the mid-1970s, a complex of factors was at work to erode the heavy restrictions placed on its entry into the major American cities. These factors included regulatory, technical, and economic considerations. In the most general terms, the regulatory system, responding to political pressure from the burgeoning cable system and sympathetic supporters, approved the implementation of technical innovations that made it feasible for the cable industry to approach markets with what were essentially new products. As a result, cable in the latter 1970s was able to begin realizing some of the envisioned potential of the late 1960s.

More specifically, the political climate became increasingly favorable to cable interests after the 1972 rule making, establishing a new context for decision making. This atmosphere was characterized by a movement away from federal regulation of the economic marketplace in all sectors. Besen and Crandall noted that Congress, by 1974, had begun hearings on deregulation of various industries, and the White House had identified excess federal regulation as a political problem and a contributor to inflation. Besen and Crandall suggested that this helped lead to the establishment by the FCC of a Cable Reregulation Task Force in 1974. The Senate issued a report in 1976 critical of the 1972 rules, and the President's Council of Economic Advisors attacked directly the FCC's restrictive cable policies.[67]

The effect of this change in attitude was a series of small but significant revisions in cable regulation in the mid-1970s. The FCC declared, for example, that cable systems could begin importing unlimited numbers of distant signals during periods when local stations were not on the air[68] and, in 1976, they were permitted to import without restriction foreign language and religious programming.[69] More significantly, the commission dropped its anti-leapfrogging rules that year, permitting cable operators to import signals from any market in the country.[70]

But while these changes were beneficial to the cable industry, the real key to growth in the major markets was the development of a truly national system of cost-efficient program distribution. For cable systems to import TV signals from beyond their normal range of reception, they had to use costly microwave relay facilities or the more primitive technique of physically shipping videotapes from one system to another. For cable to crack the major markets, a system was needed that would provide for the importation of relatively large quantities of programming at relatively low costs. The answer was the establishment of satellite distribution, and its implementation required the confluence of a number of technical, regulatory and economic events.

Until the early 1970s, communication by satellite was the domain of government owned and operated entities. But the increasing sophistication of the technology and the economic demand for more efficient methods of national and international communication led the FCC, in 1972, to adopt its so-called open skies policy of satellite regulation.[71] Under this policy, any qualified private company could build, launch, and operate a common carrier domestic satellite. Initial uses of these satellites included telephone and broadcast television service, but cable operators saw the potential as well.

In 1975, RCA launched Satcom I and, later that same year, Home Box Office (HBO) began distributing movies to cable systems using the satellite. In late 1976 the Atlanta, Georgia independent television station, WTCG, also went on the satellite, providing the first superstation service to cable operators around the country.

It took another regulatory act, however, before cable operators could economically receive these signals, for to do so required a dish antenna or ground station, the cost of which was more than most small cable operations could afford—up to $100,000.[72] Under pressure from the cable lobby, the FCC, in 1977, lowered the technical requirements for "receive only" earth stations, permitting the use of 4.5 meter dishes instead of dishes 10 meters in diameter.[73]

This reduction in dish size meant an equivalent reduction in cost to less than $25,000 and brought the satellite program delivery system within the range of most cable operators.[74] In fact, the number of systems with earth stations rose from 829 in 1978[75] to more than 2,500 in 1980.[76]

Finally, in 1977 a federal court of appeals struck down the FCC's restrictions on pay cable television, freeing HBO and similar services to offer a more attractive package to customers.[77]

Two trends thus became apparent in the mid- and latter 1970s. First, the development of a national networking system that offered at least the opportunity for cable penetration in the larger markets. Second, a movement by the federal government away from regulation of the medium.

In the first instance, the availability of new sources of programming provided cable with the leverage it needed to break into markets where previously it had little to offer potential customers in the way of alternatives to the existing broadcast station programming. Franchising activity in major markets, which had abated in the early 1970s, accelerated in the late 1970s. Subsequently, entertainment entrepreneurs saw a means of accessing a new, nationally interconnected cable audience, and a new form of program distribution began to emerge. Cable broke into the larger markets by offering movies, sports events, and additional broadcast television stations imported from other markets, plus various public service programs, through special access channels. Then, as the systems became established, independent production companies began developing programming for satellite delivery to cable operations around the country. Some of these new programming services were of a general entertainment nature; pay cable movie channels such as HBO are an example. Others took the form of very specialized programming orientations including religious, ethnic, and special interest foci. The number of these types of services rose from about three in 1976 to more than thirty by 1981. Meanwhile, the cable systems themselves were boasting channel capacities of 120 or more and cable penetration topped thirty percent with analysts of the time predicting fifty percent penetration by the end of the 1980s.

Simultaneously, the rush to deregulation continued in Washington, D.C., with the ascension to power in 1980 of a laissez-faire Republican administration. The stated intent of the new FCC Chairman, Mark Fowler, was to "unregulate" both broadcasting and cable, an aim that included repeal of the Fairness Doctrine and section 315 of the Communications Act of 1934.[78] Some members of Congress also became caught up in the deregulation movement. Senator Packwood, chairman of the Commerce Committee, held hearings on a proposed constitutional amendment to extend full First Amendment rights to the electronic media.[79]

These sentiments took more solid form in the FCC's repeal, in 1980, of the remaining regulations that most cablecasters adamantly opposed, the restrictions on distant signal importation.[80] The deletion of the rules followed a lengthy study by the FCC to determine whether a deregulated cable industry really would, as feared, create economic havoc among competing broadcasters. The commission declared such fears to be unfounded. The decision to let cable import signals from wherever it wished (given proper adherence to copyright laws) withstood a court challenge in 1981,[81] and the cable industry then moved to force repeal of what it saw as restrictive state and local regulations that had blossomed in the vacuum created by federal movement away from control.

Representatives of the cable industry attempted to repeal these regulations through federal legislation designed to override and abolish, or at least severely restrict, local controls. The political lobbying group for the nation's municipalities, the National League of Cities (NLC), strongly opposed these efforts and exerted pressure of its own for a federal bill that would formalize and legitimize local control of cable. Legislation was introduced in 1982 and again in 1983 to establish a formal national policy for cable television. Both the cable industry and the NLC played major roles in shaping that legislation, a process that culminated in 1984 with the passage of the Cable Communications Policy Act. The act represented the end product of the long and acerbic debate between the cable industry and the NLC. For the industry, the act removed the spectre of local rate regulation and limited local control over services. For the cities, it finally established federal legislative authority for local control and provided a system of franchise fees that the FCC could not dilute.[82]

The act also seemed to represent the capstone of deregulation in the cable industry. With its passage, some observers hoped that most of the local, state, and federal legislative battles over cable regulation were at an end and that most of the issues had been resolved. Subsequently, several important court cases suggested those hopes were not to be entirely fulfilled. Yet, at the time, it seemed that many of the combatants were weary of the long political struggles and would have preferred little more than to maintain the new status quo while they recuperated from the years of ferment.

In summary, cable television has moved slowly and somewhat painfully from a small-time community antenna television service to a major actor in the national communications system. Initial regulatory resistance to the technology has given way to an open market philosophy of minimum regulation. The role of the First Amendment in the process of regulation and deregulation is the next topic for consideration.

Notes

1. E. Krasnow, L. Longley and H. Terry, *The Politics of Broadcast Regulation*, 33–86 (New York: St. Martin's Press, 3d ed., 1982).

2. Inquiry into the Impact of Community Antenna Systems, TV Translators, TV Satellite Stations and TV Repeaters, on the Orderly Development of Television Broadcasting, Docket No. 12443, Report and Order, 26 F.C.C. 403 (1959); *but see,* D. LeDuc, *Cable Television and the F.C.C.: A Crisis in Media Control*, 67–68 (Philadelphia: Temple University Press, 1973) (where the roots of cable television are traced to as early as 1946).

3. *Id.*

4. R. Smith, *The Wired Nation*, 3 (New York: Harper and Row, 1972).

5. *Id.*

6. *Id.* at 46.

7. S. Head, *Broadcasting in America,* 190 (Boston: Houghton Mifflin Co., 3d ed., 1976).

8. A 1952 FCC interoffice memo appears to be the first written acknowledgment by the agency that the new CATV systems were an issue the commission might want to consider. *See* Interoffice Memorandum, March 25, 1952, reprinted in *The Television Inquiry: Review of Allocation Problems to Smaller Communities: Before the Senate Comm. on Interstate and Foreign Commerce,* 85th Cong., 2d Sess. 3490 (1958).

9. V. Mosco, *Broadcasting in the United States,* 88 (Norwood, NJ: Ablex Publishing Co., 1979).

10. *See, Licensing of Community Antenna Television Systems, Hearings Before the Senate Comm. on Interstate and Foreign Commerce,* S. Rep. No. 86-423, 86th Cong. 1st Sess. 3 (1959).

11. Broadcasters had complained to the FCC as early as 1951 about the financial effect of cable on the broadcasting business, but their concern at that time seemed limited to the issue of copyright violation. *See* F.C.C. Interoffice Memorandum, June 27, 1952, *supra* note 8, at 4124.

12. B. Compaine, *Who Owns the Media?,* 295 (New York: Harmony Books, 1979).

13. E. Krasnow and L. Longley, *The Politics of Broadcast Regulation,* 43 (New York: St. Martin's Press, 2d ed. 1978).

14. *Frontier Broadcasting v. Collier,* 24 F.C.C. 251 (1958).

15. *Id.*

16. *See, e.g.,* F.C.C. Inquiry into the Impact of CATV, *supra* note 2, at 436–37.

17. *The Television Inquiry, supra* note 8.

18. *See,* Staff of the Senate Comm. on Interstate and Foreign Commerce, 85th Cong., 2d Sess., Report on the Television Inquiry: The Problem of Television Service for Smaller Communities 46–54 (Comm. Print 1958).

19. *Broadcasting,* July 20, 1959, at 72.

20. F.C.C. Inquiry into the Impact of CATV, *supra.* 21. *VHF Booster and Community Antenna Legislation: Hearings on S. 1739, S. 1741, S. 1801, S. 1886, and S. 230 Before the Senate Comm. on Interstate and Foreign Commerce,* 86th Cong., 1st Sess. (1959).

22. S. 2653, 86th Cong. 1st Sess. (1959).

23. Smith, *supra,* at 47.

24. *See,* Memorandum and Order in Intermountain Microwave, 16 R.R. 733 (1958).

25. Carter Mountain Transmission Corp., 32 F.C.C. 459 (1962).

26. *Id.* at 464.

27. Smith, *supra,* at 45.

28. *Midwest Video Corp. v. F.C.C.,* 571 F.2d 1025, 1031 (8th Cir. 1978).

29. First Report and Order in Dockets 14985 and 15233, 38 F.C.C. 683 (1965).

30. *Id.*

31. LeDuc, *supra,* at 114–19.

32. *Id.* at 119.

33. *Id.* at 134–36.

34. Second Report and Order in Dockets 14895, 15233, and 15971, 2 F.C.C. 2d 725 (1966).

35. *Id.* at 744–45.

36. *Id.* at 772–78.

37. Smith, *supra,* at 50–51.

38. L. Ross, *Economic and Legal Foundations of Cable Television,* 17 (Beverly Hills: Sage Publications, 1974).

39. New York City was an exception, where the skyscrapers of Manhattan created sufficient interference to sustain a cable operation.

40. Krasnow, *supra,* at 43.

41. *See, e.g.,* W. Baer, *Interactive Television: Prospects for Two-Way Service on the Cable* (R-888-MF) (Santa Monica, CA: The Rand Corp., 1971); H. Dordick, et al., *Telecommunication and Urban Development* (Santa Monica, CA: The Rand Corp., 1969); Electronic Industries Association, Industrial Electronics Division, *The Future of Broadband Communication,* the IED/EIA response to the F.C.C. in Docket 18397, Part V (Washington, DC: Electronic Industries Association, 1969); National Academy of Engineering Committee on Telecommunications, *Communications Technology for Urban Development* (Washington, DC: U.S. Dept. of Commerce, 1971);

The Sloan Commission on Cable Communications, *On the Cable: The Television of Abundance* (New York: McGraw Hill, 1971); and C. Tate, *Cable Television in the Cities: Community Control, Public Access and Minority Ownership* (Washington, DC: The Urban Institute, 1971).

42. Mayor's Advisory Task Force on CATV and Telecommunications, *A Report on Cable Television and Cable Telecommunications in New York City* (1968).

43. Krasnow, *supra* note 40.

44. Smith, *supra.*

45. E. Rostow, *Final Report of the President's Task Force on Communication Policy* (Washington, DC: Government Printing Office, 1968).

46. S. Besen and R. Crandall, "*The Deregulation of Cable Television*," 44 *Law & Contemp. Probs.* 77, 94 (Winter 1981).

47. *Id.* at 96.

48. M.H. Seiden, *Cable Television U.S.A.: An Analysis of Government Policy,* 7 (New York: Praeger, 1972).

49. Besen and Crandall, *supra,* at 96.

50. *Fortnightly v. United Artists Television,* 392 U.S. 390 (1968).

51. *See, e.g.* R.E. Park, *Cable Television and UHF Broadcasting.* (R-689-MF) (Santa Monica, CA: The Rand Corp., 1971); R.E. Park, "Cable Television, UHF Broadcasting and F.C.C. Regulatory Policy," 15 *J.L. & Econ.* 207 (1972); J.J. McGowan, R.G. Noll, and M.J. Peck, *Comments Regarding the Public Interest in Commission Rules and Regulations Relating to Cable Television,* F.C.C. Docket 18397-A (Feb. 10, 1971).

52. Besen and Crandall, *supra,* at 97.

53. Notice of Proposed Rulemaking and Notice of Inquiry in Docket 18397, 15 F.C.C.2d 417 (1968).

54. Cable Television Report and Order, 36 F.C.C.2d 143 (1972).

55. First Report and Order in Docket 18397, 20 F.C.C.2d 201 (1969).

56. Second Further Notice of Proposed Rulemaking in Docket 18397-A, 24 F.C.C.2d 580 (1970).

57. Cable Television Report and Order, *supra* note 54.

58. *Id.* at 178–79.

59. *Id.* at 177–78.

60. *Id.* at 170–72.

61. *Id.* at 181–97.

62. A. Branscomb, "The Teleprompter Syndrome," mimeo (1974), *quoted in,* V. Mosco, *supra* note 9, at 100.

63. Smith, *supra,* at 62–63.

64. A. Branscomb, "The Cable Fable: Will It Come True?" 25 *J. of Communication* 44, 47 (1975).

65. *Id.*

66. *Id.* at 48.

67. Besen and Crandall, *supra,* at 98.

68. Report and Order in Docket 20028, 48 F.C.C.2d 699 (1974) and Memorandum Opinion and Order, 54 F.C.C.2d 1182 (1975).

69. First Report and Order in Docket 20553, 58 F.C.C.2d 442 (1976).

70. Report and Order in Docket 20487, 57 F.C.C.2d 625 (1976).

71. Second Report and Order in Docket 16495, 35 F.C.C.2d 844 (1972).

72. A. Hill, "CATV and Satellites: The Sky is the Limit," *Satellite Communications,* December 1978, at 20.

73. *In re* American Broadcasting Inc., 62 F.C.C.2d 901 (1977).

74. Hill, *supra,* at 24.

75. *Id.*

76. Broadcasting, June 2, 1980, at 30.

77. *Home Box Office, Inc. v. F.C.C.,* 567 F.2d 9 (D.C. Cir. 1977), *cert. denied,* 434 U.S. 829 (1978).

78. *See, e.g.,* Broadcasting, Nov. 2, 1981, at 36–37.

79. *Freedom of Expression: Hearings Held Before the Senate Comm. on Commerce, Science and Transportation,* 97th Cong., 2nd Sess. (1982). (Comm. Serial no. 97-139)

80. Cable Television Syndicated Program Exclusivity Rules and Inquiry into the Economic Relationship Between Television Broadcasting and Cable Television, 79 F.C.C.2d 663 (1980).

81. *Malrite TV v. F.C.C.,* F.2d 1140 (2d Cir. 1981), *cert. denied,* 102 S.Ct. 1002 (1982).

82. For a summary, *see* Sen. Rpt. 98-67 and House Rpt. 98-934.

3
First Amendment Issues in Cable Regulation

As chapter 2 illustrates, the regulatory history of cable television stretches back to the early 1950s and is highlighted both by the debate over whether the FCC had statutory jurisdiction to regulate and by the political influences that molded regulation once the question was settled. Of lesser prominence in decision making was the question of cable's First Amendment standing. Having suggested that the overall direction of public policy was shaped to a large extent by the popular definition of the technology, this chapter and the next seek to extend that argument to the consideration of free speech issues in cable TV. That is, it is posited that the lack of any extensive consideration of cable's First Amendment rights in early decision making and the direction of decision making that eventually did appear were the products of the dominant paradigm of cable's function and potential.

This chapter focuses on policy makers' perceptions of cable's First Amendment standing and how those perceptions affected the development of regulations at the FCC and in Congress. The subsequent chapter traces the development of this issue through the courts. Although a full appreciation of the problem must include an integrated understanding of both judicial and legislative-regulatory viewpoints, the two are divided here both for expository and substantive reasons. As will be seen, the pace of change in the two spheres is different and, therefore, they are treated separately. Further, the courts as final arbiters of First Amendment questions deserve special, rigorous examination.

The debate in Congress and at the FCC over cable's First Amendment standing can be viewed as having progressed through three distinct phases: the first characterized by a definition of cable that denied the technology as an independent form of communication, thus suppressing any discussion of free speech rights; the second resulting from a dramatic swing to a definition of cable as the true electronic forum for public expression, giving rise to a discussion of First Amendment concerns based on the rights and needs of the community; and the third phase marked by a slower recognition of potential First Amendment rights for owners and operators of the medium, as distinct from those of the public, and a definition of the technology that moved closer to a privately owned medium of communication, such as print.

CATV: Communications Medium or Antenna Service?

The View from Industry

As soon as cable started to become a thorn in the side of broadcasters—at least a perceived thorn—the discussion about possible regulation began coalescing around four major issues: (1) cable's potential status as a common carrier, (2) its potential impact on the financial health of broadcasters, (3) the problem of copyright liability, and (4) the question of local origination. A review of the earliest cable cases to come before the FCC reveals within the discussion of these issues a particular point of view by the industry as to the nature of the new enterprise. This perspective, in turn, helps explain the nature of the discussion, or lack of it, concerning cable's First Amendment position.

The first cable television question to come formally before the FCC was presented by a small cable operation in the South. J.E. Belknap and Associates filed a request with the FCC on July 1, 1951 for permission to operate two microwave stations to relay the signal of a Memphis, Tennessee television station to CATV systems in distant towns.[1] The following October, the owner of the Memphis station, WMCT, requested a hearing on the application, claiming that carriage of his signal by the CATV system would "constitute unauthorized rebroadcasts contrary to law."[2] The station owner also complained that the retransmission would violate his programming copyright.[3]

The applications filed in the Belknap case were joined by various inquiries from the public on the legal status of CATV under the Communications Act of 1934, and, in March 1952, the Common Carrier and Broadcast Bureaus of the FCC began circulating a memo suggesting rule making procedures in the issue.[4] The immediate questions, according to the memo, included whether CATV was a common carrier or broadcaster subject to commission jurisdiction and the nature of the relationship between CATV systems and the microwave links that served them.[5] The commission also was concerned, as per the WMCT request, about the property rights of broadcasters.[6] The commission studied the problem through 1953[7] and in 1954 approved the Belknap request to operate the microwave service on a common carrier basis, but took the time to point out that the decision should not be construed to imply any decision as to the FCC's authority to regulate cable.[8] There was, at this early point, no discussion of possible First Amendment issues, and the decision of the commission to permit operation militated against their development.

Similarly, the FCC's subsequent 1956 decision in *Frontier Broadcasting v. Collier* to decline regulation failed to provide an initial setting for a 1950s constitutional challenge.[9] As in the Belknap case, *Frontier* offered an early opportunity for cable, broadcast, and governmental interests to express their views about the relationship between the new technology and the government. But the debate failed to generate concerns about freedom of expression.

The FCC's decision not to assert jurisdiction in *Frontier* resulted, as previously noted, in broadcasters taking their case to Congress.

In hearings before both congressional and regulatory panels, therefore, industry representatives were confronted with a situation in which a constitutional argument could have been raised to rebut efforts to invoke federal regulation. But a review of the testimony at those early hearings reveals that at no time did any of the parties raise substantial questions about the constitutionality of regulation. In fact, the tactics used by the industry in these early hearings discouraged use of a First Amendment shield.

Specifically, cable interests focused on two of the major policy questions—the possibility of cable's being regulated as a common carrier and the problem of cable's effect on local broadcasters—and instead of addressing potential constitutional problems, directly challenged the assumptions of the positions. In a lengthy brief submitted during 1958 Senate Commerce Committee hearings, spokesmen for the industry pointed out the functional differences between CATV and a common carrier, an argument similar to the one used successfully in the FCC hearings in *Frontier*.[10] With respect to any significant financial impact on broadcasting, cable operators simply denied such potential existed. Representatives of the National Cable Television Association (NCTA) told the hearing that complaints of economic harm came only from a few ailing broadcasters looking for a scapegoat for economic problems caused by various other factors.[11]

The cable industry's response to complaints and requests for regulation, therefore, was no broader than the original charge. CATV interests could attack the arguments directly without recourse to sweeping constitutional rhetoric. But would they have raised the constitutional defense if it had seemed appropriate? A review of the NCTA position on the two other major regulatory matters—copyright and local origination—suggests not.

The industry did not try to argue the copyright question out of existence as it had the economic and common carrier issues. It conceded that there was an honest difference of opinion with broadcasters about compensation for program material.[12] The industry instead sought to circumvent the issue definitionally by attempting to convince legislators and regulators that CATV was nothing more than a master antenna service, a functional extension of the subscriber's television set. When asked whether CATV violated section 325 of the Communications Act,[13] which prohibits the retransmission of television signals, NCTA attorney E. Stratford Smith told the Senate investigating committee:

> There again, the community antenna system is not engaged in rebroadcasting. It is a reception service; it is a master antenna facility, and therefore, in my opinion, not covered by Section 325 of the Communications Act.[14]

To the extent that rights were involved, they were, according to Smith, the rights of the viewers to obtain public TV through a master antenna system:[15]

> The community antenna system operator is receiving signals that go into the homes of the public. The public leases an antenna service from him. The community antenna operator is not selling the program; he is selling an antenna service, and the performance is a private performance in the home by people who have a right to receive television programs that have been broadcast to the public.[16]

By declaring CATV to be a service for hire, the industry removed itself from all control of and responsibility for the content of the system beyond simply selecting the channels. There was no retransmission, no communication medium conceptually separable from the viewer's rabbit ears.

As a tactic for avoiding copyright liability, is was an ingenious and eventually successful proposal,[17] but it was indicative of a view of cable television that prevented the early development of a strong First Amendment position for the industry. Without a functional definition as a medium of communication—a system with editorial discretion—the CATV operator could claim no constitutional protection under the free speech clause for there was essentially nothing to protect.

Finally, the concept of CATV as an independent communications system might have been developed through discussion of the constitutional role of local origination. Programming originated by the cable operator certainly could not be considered passive in the same sense as broadcast signal carriage, nor could it be justified on the basis of scarcity. The operator might have invoked a First Amendment protection on the basis of this form of message propagation. Such was not the case, however. The industry took great pains to downplay any consideration of local origination, for it apparently saw the service as politically vulnerable. Both the application and success of local origination were, therefore, minimized. In the 1958 hearings, Smith told committee members that there were "some instances in which community antenna operators [had] experimented, through a separate company or separate legal entity, with closed-circuit programming on an extra or spare channel," but that in almost every case the experiment was a financial failure and not likely to be continued.[18]

The industry was sensitive to complaints from broadcasters about potential competition in this area, and one successful cable operator at the time told policymakers that the NCTA had actively discouraged its members from beginning local origination in order to avoid such competition.[19]

In short, the industry attempted to remove the question of local origination from the broader debate over cable regulation, but, in doing so, it also removed the mechanism through which constitutional issues might have been formulated at this stage.

The manner in which CATV was presented to policymakers by the industry itself, therefore, only helped prevent the development of the question of cable rights in the 1950s.

The View from Congress and the FCC

The FCC's early definitional approach to CATV considered only the system's ability to pick signals out of the air and retransmit them; no additional communicative functions were considered.[20]

This view paralleled the one advanced by the industry itself with one important exception: Whereas the industry promoted CATV as an adjunct to the viewer's home antenna, and, therefore, exempt from regulation, the government tended to perceive CATV as an adjunct to the broadcast system, an extension of the transmitting antenna, and, therefore, subject to the authority of at least Congress, if not the FCC.

As FCC deliberation over the question of CATV continued into the mid and late 1950s, it became apparent that, whether or not the commission could invoke technical jurisdiction, it saw the new technology as an extension of and an element within the system of national broadcasting. As such it was considered in the 1959 Inquiry along with TV boosters, translators, and satellite stations as an auxiliary service to broadcasting.[21]

CATV was seen in the first instance as a rather neutral, passive service which did little to produce its own messages and was, therefore, an extension of the broadcasting system over which the FCC did command authority. The language of the law had created a loophole by which cable had slipped away from commission jurisdiction, but this was considered, at bottom, a legislative oversight. There were, for the commission, no constitutional questions here. As there were no First Amendment barriers to its regulation of broadcasting, it was inconceivable that there could be any First Amendment barriers to government regulation of broadcasting's auxiliary services. With this proposition as the starting point, constitutional questions in early decision

making were foreclosed. The FCC could, as it did, seek formal jurisdiction over CATV from Congress without concern for the First Amendment.

In response, Congress seemed, at least for a time, most anxious to help since the definition of cable TV was such that First Amendment issues were never raised. Like the FCC, congressional policymakers grouped CATV among the other auxiliary services. In summarizing the 1958 Senate hearings on the problems of CATV, then Commerce Committee staff member Kenneth Cox (later an FCC Commissioner) stated:

> It seems clear that the Commission should have, and should vigorously exercise, regulatory power over all these alternative means of bringing television service to the public. It is difficult to see how the Commission can perform its duties to the public and effectuate the will of Congress without such broad and inclusive authority, because, as it pointed out [in this report], these various services interact with each other in many ways. It is unfair to impose standards of public service on part of those who furnish television service to the public while leaving others similarly engaged free of all such obligations. It seems quite clear that the overall television industry cannot thrive and grow to the greatest ultimate public interest, if it continues to exist only half regulated.[22]

The sentiments of the committee reflected in the staff report were reified in legislative proposals the following year. Senate Bill 2653, the cable regulation bill, included virtually every clause affecting and controlling the broadcast industry.[23] It proposed direct application of everything from construction permits to content regulations such as equal time and fairness.[24]

In examining the congressional and regulatory activities of the 1950s, one sees a preponderance of time and energy spent on discussions and analyses of CATV's economic impact on broadcasters and the issue of telecaster property rights. But it is apparent that discussions about the constitutionality of congressional or FCC authority over the new medium of communication never arose because CATV simply was not defined as a new medium of communication. There was no medium in the sense of a separate communicator or system of communications and, so, nothing to which First Amendment rights could be attached.

The industry presented itself, at least for political purposes, as an extension of the home viewer's antenna. The government, when it characterized CATV at all, leaned toward defining it as a relatively passive extension of the broadcasting service. In taking these somewhat different perspectives on CATV, cable, government, and industry were setting the stage for a confrontation that later would take on constitutional proportions, but as of the late 1950s, that confrontation was not yet envisioned.

The Model in Transition: Early Constitutional Challenges

The death of S. 2653 in 1960 marked the end of serious legislative consideration of cable, and, hence, the end of potential debate in Congress over the constitutional merits of CATV until 1966. While cable regulation bills were introduced in several sessions in the interim, no substantial action was taken.[25]

FCC activity in the area also slackened. With the exception of the important Carter Mountain decision, in which no constitutional or content questions were considered, the commission did little with the medium.

The first real debates over the constitutional standing of CATV and the government's overall role in regulating cable content came, as could be expected, only with the first application of comprehensive rules growing out of the commission's 1965[26] and 1966 CATV decisions.[27]

The issuance of those regulations and the FCC's concurrent request for congressionally approved jurisdiction gave rise to two separate but philosophically related debates of the constitutional question, one within the FCC itself and one within Congress. Both were important, for they addressed for the first time outside the courts.[28] the constitutional problems of applying broadcast-like regulations to a nonbroadcast medium. Further, they illustrated the shift of the cable industry in its position on the constitutional issue. Its arguments against government control having failed to halt implementation of jurisdiction, cable firms turned to the First Amendment defense, probably out of practical as much as philosophical considerations. Government, reasoned cablecasters, had brought control to an industry deeply involved in the communications process and, therefore, the constitutional argument was at least one necessary element in their stand against such intrusion.

The Debate at the FCC

The first such case to come before the commission arose as a direct challenge to its constitutional authority to implement the 1966 Second Report and Order, and it provided a clear exposition of the commission's views at that time on the nature of cable television. In enforcing the 1966 order, the FCC had issued a cease and desist notice against a Pennsylvania cable system that was carrying TV signals in violation of the newly established rules.[29] The cable operator, Back Mountain Telecable, Inc., and the community it served, Kingston, Pennsylvania, challenged the order and requested a hearing on the constitutional authority of the commission to issue the regulations. The cable company claimed an unconstitutional infringement on its right to free speech, and the community claimed a similar infringement on the right of its citizens to receive information.[30]

The request for an oral argument was denied and the constitutional issues brushed aside by a majority of the commission in a terse, one-paragraph proclamation that the questions raised in the case had been disposed of in the Second Report and Order itself.[31] The FCC then called upon three cases— *N.B.C. v. U.S.*,[32] *Carter Mountain*,[33] and *Idaho Microwave, Inc. v. F.C.C.*[34]— in support of its position, concluding, "No purpose would be served by oral argument" over the issue.[35]

This summary dismissal of the problem was attacked in a pointed dissent by Commissioner Lee Loevinger.[36] He correctly noted that the sections of the Second Report and Order cited by the majority did not address any constitutional issues but rather dealt only with interpretation of various statutes. More importantly, Loevinger, for the first time in published FCC debate, pointed out that the commission's authority over enterprises involving broadcasting might not extend to an industry not dependent on the propagation of radio waves.

> [A]ll three cases cited (*N.B.C.*, *Carter Mountain* and *Idaho*) involved the Commission's authority over enterprises involved in radio transmission and subject to the licensing power of the Commission. The present case involves an order requiring cessation of operation by an intrastate enterprise making no radio transmissions and not subject to the Commission's licensing authority.[37]

At least, he argued, the commission should not have so quickly dismissed consideration of the issue.

This first brief skirmish between Loevinger and his fellow commissioners subsequently exploded into a full-scale battle when the commission issued an opinion in 1967 rejecting several requests that had been filed by the cable industry for reconsideration of the 1966 Order.[38] Whereas the Back Mountain case limited its constitutional assault to the Cease and Desist Order, this new Petition for Reconsideration sought total rescission of the 1966 rules, in part on First Amendment grounds. The commission commented more fully here on the constitutional issues, but the outcome was no different than that in Back Mountain. Said the majority:

> It is well established that reasonable regulation of radio transmissions, if consistent with the public interest as that term is defined taking into account the overall purposes and provisions of the act, is not violative of the right of free speech. This principle has been applied to the imposition of carriage and nonduplication restrictions on CATV similar to those finally adopted in the Second Report and Order.[39]

As in Back Mountain, the commission called upon *N.B.C., Carter Mountain,* and *Idaho Microwave* to support its position, going on to clarify the use of those cases by explaining:

> While it is true that those cases dealt with radio licensing, we have now held that CATV's provide an extension of a broadcast service. If, as we believe, Congress has given us the regulatory authority we have asserted, there is no reason why the free speech principles should apply differently to those CATV's which derive their signals off-the-air than to those which use licensed radio.[40]

The majority opinion concluded that CATV had no more constitutional right to extend broadcast service into an area than a broadcaster had to increase the height and power of an antenna in violation of the public interest.[41] In other words, the FCC was applying its definition of cable as an extension of broadcasting to the question of constitutionally permissible control. If its authority over broadcasting was constitutional, so must be its authority over CATV, it reasoned.

In dissent, Loevinger took a very different view of the situation, separating the media both conceptually and constitutionally:

> It should be self-evident from the Supreme Court statement (in *N.B.C.*) that, contrary to the position of the instant opinion, there is every reason "why free speech principles should apply differently" to those CATVs which do not use radio transmissions and to those which do. The whole reason and rationale for regulation in this field is the physical necessity for establishing and maintaining technical standards and order so that radio transmission is possible. Further, the rationale of the *N.B.C.* case is based squarely and solely on the necessity of denying access to radio transmission to some because of the limited space in the spectrum. It makes no legal, technical or logical sense to say that a case holding regulation to be justified because of the "limited facilities of radio" transmission also justifies the same regulation of cable.[42]

Loevinger went on to suggest that by the continued extension of its arguments, the FCC could assert "that 'there is no reason why the free speech principles should apply differently' to newspapers than to radio merely because the situation involving the technical mode of communication is different."[43] He said that the FCC could, thereby, claim jurisdiction over newspapers, magazines, and motion pictures.

Rebutting Loevinger, Commissioner Kenneth Cox repeated the contention that CATV was merely a "part of the scheme of broadcasting."[44] Cox said that "unlike any other purely nonbroadcast mode of expression," radio signals were essential to cable's livelihood. "Therefore," he concluded, "their reasonable regulation to prevent frustration of the congressional scheme for our broadcast service does not violate the First Amendment."[45]

The exchanges in these two cases clearly illustrate the FCC's early position on CATV. They also signaled the start of real debate over the validity of that position. Meanwhile, a similar process of debate and reevaluation was taking place in Congress.

The Debate within Congress

The point of departure for the congressional consideration of CATV's constitutional standing was the problem of local origination. As previously noted, the commission's confidence in its role as regulator of "CATV, the TV retransmission device" did not carry over into similar confidence about its role as regulator of "CATV, independent message transmitter", and, when the commission asked Congress to clarify its jurisdiction over cable, following the Second Report and Order, it also asked for authority to control local origination.[46]

This request served as a springboard for a 1966 congressional consideration of the question about content control of cable-originated programming and cable's constitutional status.[47] The House Committee on Interstate and Foreign Commerce took testimony on the issue from representatives of the cable industry, which was more conciliatory before the House than it had been before the FCC, perhaps seeing some regulatory legislation as inevitable and hoping to soften the impact through negotiated compromise. While NCTA President Frederick Ford argued that the Constitution prevented the government from restricting local origination totally, he had no objection to the application of broadcastlike content controls.[48] This position was consistent with the industry's earlier attempts to define cable as an antenna service, and it appeared to be a position acceptable to most members of the committee, which reported out a bill that would have prohibited "the origination of program or other material by a CATV system with such limitations or exceptions, if any, as are deemed appropriate (by the F.C.C.)."[49] Paralleling the FCC hearings, however, a minority report was issued attacking the position of the majority on constitutional grounds. The minority stated flatly that the proposed legislation "would violate the constitutional guarantees of the First Amendment."[50] It went on to question the rationale for regulation of cable in general, noting the absence of a scarcity argument and stating with respect to the limitation on local origination:

> In no community in the United States would the people have the freedom to receive over a CATV system any local program of weather, information, news P.T.A. meetings, town council meetings, civil defense or other emer-

gency information, or any other matter not approved by the Federal Communications Commission in Washington, D.C.[51]

The proposed legislation died in the Rules Committee, but apparently not as a result of the constitutional questions. The minority views in the Commerce Committee and at the FCC notwithstanding, the definition of cable as an adjunct to broadcasting with only limited constitutional protection seemed well-entrenched. On the other hand, the opposition opinions indicated the beginning of a change in that definition of cable that soon would bring questions of content control to the forefront.

The People's Medium

During the early and mid-1960s, the technical capacity of CATV was increasing. For the first ten years of its existence, it had been limited to carrying about three to six channels, but technical improvements in the second ten years doubled that potential and promised greater increases in the future. Through at least 1966, the FCC failed to see the potential of this expanded cable system as a means of increasing community access to information and of increased opportunity for expression. The commission and Congress were blinded by a definition of CATV that was shaped by its relationship to broadcasting, and within the context of that relationship, CATV's increased potential was seen only as the potential to wreak economic havoc on local broadcasters.

But as pointed out in chapter 2 and suggested in the dissents of Loevinger and the House Minority Report, that definition was becoming subject to increased questioning. The passive view of cable was being altered in the middle and late 1960s and by the early 1970s had changed radically. Two reports—Mayor Lindsay's New York Task Force report and the paper by the President's Task Force on Cable—were particularly influential. The former, in fact, was quoted at length by the FCC in its 1968 Notice of Inquiry into additional rule making in the CATV area. Said the commission:

> It has been suggested [by the Task Force] that the expanding multichannel capacity of cable systems could be utilized to provide a variety of new communications services to homes and businesses within a community, in addition to the services now commonly offered, such as time, weather, news, stock exchange ticker, etc.[52]

In addition, Smith's book, the Sloan Commission Report, the Rand Studies, and a multitude of articles in the popular press increasingly worked to change the public perception of cable. The press praised cable's potential as the communication system of the future and forecast services ranging from job training to electronic mail delivery. Among cable's benefits, according to the researchers and critics, were the expansion of the political and cultural marketplace of ideas, and new opportunities for freedom of expression. The Sloan Commission, for example, exclaimed that:

> [T]he copiousness of cable television makes it possible to conceive of far broader access to its channels by competing entrepreneurs and hence opens up the possibilities of a far broader expression of opinion. The existence of public access channels and the recommendations this Commission will make concerning their general availability and the principles governing their use, will make possible the expression of an extraordinary range of opinion, in practice as well as in principle.[53]

Through the evolution of the technology, the First Amendment question began to seep into the cable debate as an attribute of the medium, and both the change in perspective and the new role of freedom of expression in the debate found their way into federal policy making. In this regard, 1968 appears to have been the watershed year. The FCC's use of the New York Task Force report has been noted; additional evidence comes in the FCC's Annual Reports. Prior to 1968, the annual report—a summary of the commission's activities for that year—officially described cable simply as a system that "receives and amplifies the transmission of TV broadcast stations and then redistributes the signals by wire or cable to subscribers for a fee."[54]

To this description, however, the commission's 1968 report added, for the first time, the observation that cable could

> offer specialized services, reserving separate channels for weather, stock market and wire service news reports. Some cable operators produce their own programs, offering coverage of city council meetings and other local events. The potential uses of CATV are still being explored. What was originally conceived as a mere multiple-channel reception device may develop into a home communications center enabling subscribers to shop from their armchairs for merchandise shown on their TV screen, order facsimile newspapers, or have their meters read—all through a cable connected to their TV sets.[55]

In short, policymakers, succumbing to the changing paradigm of cable TV, began to ponder methods of forging the new medium into a vehicle for the advancement of the community's interest in freedom of expression. Early impetus for formal consideration of the issue came once again in the area of local program origination.

In 1968, a broadcaster in San Diego, California, asked the FCC to ban local cable operators from importing signals from Los Angeles and to pre vent them from originating their own programmming.[56] In Midwest Television, Inc., the commission granted, in part, the request on signal importation, but denied the plea to halt the origination programming. Such origination, explained the commission, served the public interest by providing an additional outlet for local expression.[57]

In its decision, the commission took great pains to affirm its authority to regulate local origination if it chose, noting that no First Amendment barriers existed to such regulations since they furthered the community's interest in expression.[58] The commission's comments also revealed its growing awareness of the potential benefit of cable to the community-at-large and to minority interests in particular. The concept of local origination became, in fact, so attractive to the commission that, a few months after the Midwest decision, it issued a Notice of Proposed Rulemaking to consider making origination channels mandatory for all cable systems.[59]

The local origination rules were subsequently adopted for systems with more than 3,500 subscribers,[60] but were never implemented. Court challenges[61] and the massive 1968-to-1972 rule-making procedures directed policy away from origination and toward access, which many began perceiving as the final solution to the problem of freedom of expression in cable television. Even in its 1969 order mandating origination, the commission implied the ultimate benefits of access:

> The most marked potential of the cable technology for enhancing communication services to the public stems from its expanding channel capacity. . . . From a diversity standpoint, it seems beyond dispute that one party should not control the content of communications on so many channels into the home. For it has long been a basic tenet of national communications policy that "the widest possible dissemination of information from diverse and antagonistic sources is essential to the welfare of the public."[62]

The new concept of cable as a public service was thus extended in 1972 with the formal implementation of public and leased access channels.[63] Not only were cable systems to make channels available for public use, but systems in the top 100 markets were required to provide studio facilities for groups requesting access to the special channels.[64]

The 1972 rules also included the restrictions on distant signal importation, which would seem to work against the FCC's support of diversity in cable. But the commission circumvented this argument by claiming that importation of such signals did not represent true diversity, since most TV fare was of the same network-generated mold and thus

> the diversity gained by cumulative broadcast signals is largely a matter of choice of viewing time, rather than any real additional choice in terms of new or different programming. We believe that much more significant ad-

ditional choice of programming is likely to be achieved in the long run if some cable channels are devoted to program origination.[65]

Cable operators, of course, perceived the restrictions on signal importation as a significant imposition on their First Amendment rights. While the access channel requirements illustrated the change in FCC perception about cable and its role in freedom of expression, the restriction on signal carriage became the focal point for debate at the FCC on cable's First Amendment status following the 1972 Report and Order.

Numerous system owners sought a waiver of the rules so they could import distant signals, and quite often the petition for a waiver was accompanied by arguments that the regulations themselves were violative of the First Amendment protection of free speech. What is interesting about these cases is not the FCC denial of most of the waivers, but the shift in the rhetoric used by the commission to rebut the constitutional argument and support its authority over the medium.

In similar cases following the imposition of the 1966 rules, the commission, as previously noted, argued that cable was an extension of broadcasting and therefore subject to broadcastlike regulation. But in keeping with the change in the definitional paradigm, all the language supporting the commission's authority based on the early criteria disappeared in the cases in the early 1970s. Instead, the commission turned to the broader justification of "enhancing First Amendment goals of diversity" and "integrating cable into national communications policy."[66]

The first such case to come before the commission following imposition of the 1972 rules was In Re: Daniels Properties, Inc.[67] A cable operator in Nolanville, Texas requested a waiver of signal carriage rules to import two TV stations from Dallas. Among several arguments marshaled by the operator in support of the application was the contention that the rules as applied in this situation violated the free press clause of the First Amendment by "preventing some cable subscribers from receiving information."[68] But the FCC rejected the argument, countering that, taken in their entirety, the broader goal of FCC rules was to advance the interests of the First Amendment even though specific rules may, in isolated instances, restrict the availability of programming to some. Said the FCC:

> The Commission also has a broad responsibility with respect to the First Amendment, which is to actively foster the flow of ideas and information through the broadcast media to all of the people. This responsibility has long been recognized as important enough to justify regulations which promote diversity of expression generally, but which may, in particular instances, have an effect on the content of available programming.[69]

Interestingly, the decision does not refer to cable either as an extension or an ancillary service of broadcasting, underscoring the shift in regulatory perceptions of and rationales for the regulation of the new medium.

The commission's constitutional defense was expanded and refined a bit in a subsequent case, In Re. Cable Systems, Inc.[70] Here, the cable operator petitioned for waiver of signal carriage requirements but used a broader argument than that offered in Daniels. It claimed the FCC's rules, in general, were unconstitutional on their face, rather than simply as applied in this particular situation. As in the Daniels case, however, the FCC rejected the argument, repeating the logic of that earlier case. It also responded to an argument by the cable company that the precedent used by the commission to defend its position was incorrectly based on cases stemming from the 1966 rules rather than the new regulations of the 1970s.[71]

Although it admitted a difference between the rules considered in the 1960s and those at hand, the commission concluded that the distinction was immaterial since

> both sets of rules are grounded in common policy considerations deriving from the Communications Act of 1934 the orderly integration of cable television into the national communications structure and in each instance the commission was attempting to fashion a signal carriage program with the least possible restrictions on alleged First Amendment freedoms without any intent to suppress free expression. See *United States v. O'Brien,* 391 U.S. 367 (1968).[72]

The reference to *O'Brien* is interesting here. In that case, the Supreme Court decided that the jailing of a draft card burner did not violate the First Amendment, for, although the act may have had some communicative value, its suppression was only incidental to the broader governmental goal of maintaining an orderly system of draft registration.[73] The use of the case, therefore, is tacit admission that the rules did violate some First Amendment values, even though those values might be secondary to the broader concerns of the commission. Further, it reinforced the notion that such abridgment was permissible so long as the action of the state is directed at achieving a larger social good, in this case a countervailing interest in the First Amendment itself, defined here, in part, as the melding of the cable service into the nation's communication system.[74]

The only other relevant exchange in this line of decisions was In Re. Tulsa Cable Television in 1978[75] when the cable operator in question used a recent appeals court decision[76]—striking down FCC rules on pay cable— to challenge the signal carriage regulations. In the appeals court case, *H.B.O. v. F.C.C.,* the court suggested that there was little constitutional justification for FCC authority over cable television.[77] But the commission responded to this only in a brief footnote, dismissing the decision as irrelevant to the case at hand due to the difference between the question of retransmission and the question of origination programming. According to the commission,[78] the two functions could be separated conceptually and, therefore, dealt with differently under the law. There was, however, much in the appeals court decisions implying skepticism about the commission's authority to regulate signal importation, and making its use of this distinction, at best, a strained interpretation of the ruling. Nonetheless, it underscored the commission's determination to maintain its authority over cable television despite the unfavorable court decision, and it did not deter the commission from using earlier, favorable cases as precedents for regulating cable in the public interest.[79]

Following the Tulsa case, several other constitutional challenges were mounted in signal importation questions, but none displayed any new facets or suggested novel arguments.[80] All presented straightforward claims that the rules violated the First Amendment, and all were dismissed with identical and seemingly standard recitations of the earlier court cases upholding FCC authority, with the explanation that the Commission was attempting to fashion a signal carriage program "with the least possible restrictions on First Amendment freedom and without any intent to suppress free expression."[81] The repetition of the language in these latter cases strongly suggested that the commission had given up serious consideration of the issues, although the discussion may have been unenthusiastic in anticipation of the probable elimination of the importation rules.[82] It may have been indicative of the increasingly fashionable trend toward deregulation and the new perception of cable television that accompanied that trend.

A First Amendment Right for Cablecasters

Taken in isolation, the above cases could be interpreted as an argument that the definition of cable television as primarily a public service or public utility retained its currency through the middle and latter 1970s. But a reading of related regulatory rule making and congressional debate shows that this is probably not the case, and the decisions reflect perhaps only the commission's desire to protect its rules while a new path was being surveyed.

In fact, the general drift toward deregulation following the 1972 Report and Order suggested gradual abandonment of the public service model and an inching away from what might have been considered a public communications resource. The apparent retreat from this concept was, no doubt, inspired by the political realities of the broader trend toward deregulation of all industries. But there are indications that a growing governmental awareness of the practical problems of the industry also was influential.

It can be argued that the concept of CATV as a panacea for the ills of society in general and the major cities in particular was a partial product of the so-called Blue Sky era of the middle and late 1960s. Given this argument, the logical effect of a decline or death of the visions held then would, in part, be a retreat from the belief in cable's social service potential. Cable's general financial and industrial troubles in the early and middle 1970s have been recounted in chapter 2. Evidence that these problems translated into regulatory action can be seen in the explanations that accompanied several FCC decisions of that time.

In rescinding its local origination requirements, for example, the commission admitted that the rules would work a hardship on some smaller operations.[83] The commission also conceded in 1975 that its rules requiring some systems to rebuild to meet channel capacity and access guidelines of the 1972 Order might have overestimated the industry's resources and abilities.[84] Following its task force inquiry, the commission voided the rebuild requirements, estimating that the change saved the industry up to $430 million.[85]

The 1976 rules predicated access channels on the basis of system rather than market size, a measure more likely to reflect the ability of the cable operator to afford the change. In explaining the change, the commission recalled its desire to provide new outlets for local expression, but also stated that such "abstract notions of public good must be carefully tested as to their cost and practical, realistic impact.[86]

In short, the definition of what cable could do—what cable was—had become more realistic; yet, at the same time, it had become less certain. No longer was there a unifying definition, an overarching viewpoint about CATV to guide decision making with respect to First Amendment issues. The problem was compounded by the evolution of the industry itself as it moved out of its economic malaise at the end of the 1970s. Where the 1950s had seen cable equated with an extension of the broadcaster and the later 1960s a public communications resource not unlike a grand video telephone exchange, the 1970s provided no such parallel. In fact, cable moved away from both analogies by developing a strong ration of its own programming. As previously noted, new cable networks based on specialized, targeted audiences grew at a tremendous rate from 1978 to 1982. On systems with channel capacities of 50 or 100, fewer than 10 or 15 were devoted to the retransmission of traditional broadcast signals or local public access. Cable was no longer a total captive of the broadcast system, nor was it the realization of a dream of political and cultural self-actualization or community unification. It had become a unique medium with special characteristics, apparently lacking analogy to older technologies.

At the same time, any search for a conceptual definition to facilitate regulation at the federal level was frustrated by the deregulatory movement;

it was unnecessary to have a core philosophy of cable expression if rules regarding cable were being repealed. The marketplace, it was believed, would supply natural parameters; legal definitions seemed unnecessary.

There were attempts to develop a comprehensive framework for the control of cable in the 1970s, but they created more rhetoric than action. A 1976 House subcommittee staff report, for example, urged elimination of most controls on cable content and adoption of a separations policy that would have imposed upon cable the status of a full common carrier.[87] The report, which was highly critical of the FCC's handling of cable, served as the basis for subcommittee hearings on CATV policy, but no legislation resulted from these hearings.[88]

Another failed attempt at comprehensive regulations began in 1977 with a lengthy Congressional report on electronic communication, written to provide a starting point for congressional deliberations on the rewrite of the Communications Act of 1934.[89] This Option Papers report outlined a variety of ways to deal with cable that its authors claimed would accommodate all legitimate interests, but after several years of hearings, the rewrite attempt died in the face of industry opposition.

Unfortunately for national regulators, state and local governments were only too glad to enter in where senators and congressmen feared to tread. As the FCC began releasing cable companies from years of control, local agencies—and occasionally states—stepped into the regulatory vacuum. At the same time, the cable industry, having won much of its regulatory fight at the federal level, turned its political attention to solving what it saw as a continuing and now, perhaps, growing problem of legal constraint by non-federal agencies. The cable companies perceived the local franchising agencies—cities and towns—as the last great barriers to full deregulation and began lobbying efforts to limit local control. The mechanism they chose was federal legislation that would force the states and cities to do what the federal government had done voluntarily: get out of the business of regulating cable. As noted in the previous chapter, the industry's efforts were challenged by the National League of Cities, which saw the possibility of losing a substantial source of local income in the form of franchise fees if cities lost the power to closely monitor the franchises. The battle lines were, thus, drawn, and the fierce debate over the implementation of a national cable policy proceeded through the early 1980s.

A series of bills to deregulate broadcasting were considered, and comprehensive legislation was eventually passed by Congress.[90] There were attempts to attach cable amendments to the bills, but those efforts failed, in part, because of congressional concern that the proposed broadcast regulation was sufficiently complex without throwing cable into the pot.[91] Separate legislation tailored to meet the cable problem was introduced in 1982.[92] Through the volatile process of negotiation between NLC and NCTA a bill satisfactory to both sides eventually was delivered and by 1984 was passed by Congress.[93]

Resolution of the legislative debate did not, however, imply resolution of the constitutional debate; the problem of cable's First Amendment status was illustrated by the legislative process but not solved by it. During hearings on the cable bills, in their various forms, spokespersons from all constitutional perspectives pleaded their case.[94] The cities predictably argued an implicit definition of cable as an important forum for the exchange of ideas that ought to be maintained for the people by the local government.[95] The industry, just as predictably, argued that cable was merely one of many possible sources of information in a system abundant with communications channels and that regulation based on a restricted market view was not in keeping with marketplace realities.[96]

Final passage of the bill did not illuminate the question substantially. For the first time, a congressional definition of cable as a two-way communications medium was adopted, and Congress declared that cable was not to be considered a public utility.[97] But the nature of cable's constitutional status was left as muddled as it was when the bills were first introduced. Even within the Senate and House reports on the cable legislation the dispute continued. The two ideologically opposed committees presented, for legislative history, two very different pictures of what they saw as cable's potential in facilitating a First Amendment forum.

This difference was particularly sharp in the debate over whether the legislation should call for mandatory public access channels. Did a requirement giving the public free access to the system advance the First Amendment interests of the community or violate the First Amendment rights of the cablecaster? The committees approached the question from divergent perspectives.

The report of the House committee spoke to the longstanding vision of cable as an outlet for community voices, defending the access requirements as not only in keeping with but advancing the purposes of the First Amendment:

> The committee is aware that access provisions have been challenged in the courts as inconsistent with the First Amendment rights of the cable operator. The committee believes, nonetheless, that the access provisions contained in this legislation are consistent with and further the goals of the First Amendment. The provisions established a form of content-neutral structural regulation which will foster the availability of a "diversity of viewpoints" to the listening audience.[98]

The more conservative Senate committee, on the other hand, went along with the access requirements only with the greatest reluctance and misgivings. It did not share the House's concerns about cable's role as a First Amendment forum: "The committee firmly believes in encouraging competition and not imposing any regulation where marketplace forces are better able to insure innovation, diversity and efficiency."[99]

This belief in the ability of market forces to solve any First Amendment problem was the tool with which the committee could conceptually shape cable into a private and independent medium with implicitly strong First Amendment guarantees against government control. The committee suggested that only the lack of maturity of potential communications competitors compelled the acceptance of the access channel proposals, and that once those competitors had matured, the rationale for access would dissipate, with access requirements themselves following similarly.[100]

The theoretical problem of cable's First Amendment standing was not resolved by either the discussions about or passage of the Cable Communications Policy Act, although the process may have somewhat sharpened the positions. Of course, the act itself could be questioned on First Amendment grounds. It was, after all, a framework for federal control over an important medium of expression that was not soundly grounded, and thereby rationalized, in First Amendment theory. On the other hand, there was some initial expectation that passage of the act might forestall new judicial consideration of the problem, as the industry—having satisfied itself in Congress—would not seek further gains in the courts. But such hopes were short-lived as several cases quickly arose in which the constitutionality of the Act itself—or parts of it—was, in fact, the question.

In summary, First Amendment concerns have played an important part in the development of regulatory and legislative policymaking. Many of the dimensions of the debate have evolved in these forums. To that extent, the discussions within Congress and the FCC about cable's constitutional standing have contributed substantially to the shaping of policy and, hence, the structure of the industry. Still, the legislative and regulatory bodies do not determine constitutional questions. So, while not dismissing the practical effect of the interim constitutional policy forged there, it must be noted that this area is the ultimate purview of the courts. Judicial perceptions of the First Amendment status of cable will, in the end, be definitive, and so we now turn our discussion toward those perceptions.

Notes

1. Memorandum Opinion and Order in the matter of Belknap and Associates, 18 F.C.C. 642 (1954).

2. F.C.C. Interoffice Memorandum, June 27, 1952, *reprinted in The Television Inquiry: Review of Allocation Problems of TV Service to Smaller Communi-*

ties: Hearings Before the Senate Comm. on Interstate and Foreign Commerce, 85th Cong., 2nd Sess., pt. 6, 4124 (1958).

3. *Id.*

4. *Id* at 3490.

5. *Id.*

6. F.C.C. Interoffice Memorandum, *supra* note 2, at 4123–24.

7. *F.C.C. Annual Report 1953,* at 34.

8. Belknap, *supra.*

9. 24 F.C.C. 251 (1958).

10. *The Television Inquiry, supra* note 2, at 3813–30.

11. *Id.* at 3789.

12. *Id.*

13. 47 U.S.C. sec. 325(a) (1962).

14. *The Television Inquiry, supra* note 2, at 3792.

15. *Id.* at 3789.

16. *Id.* at 3791.

17. *See Fortnightly Corp. v. United Artists,* 392 U.S. 390 (1968).

18. *The Television Inquiry, supra* note 2 at 3792–93.

19. *VHF Booster and Community Antenna Television Legislation: Hearings Before the Senate Comm. on Interstate and Foreign Commerce,* 86th Cong., 1st Sess., 682 (1959) (testimony of New York cable operator Milton Shapp).

20. *FCC Annual Report,* at 33–34 (1953).

21. Inquiry into the Impact of Community Antenna Systems, TV Translators, TV Satellite Stations, and TV Repeaters on the Orderly Development of Television Broadcasting, Docket 12443, 26 F.C.C. 403 (1959).

22. Staff of the Senate Comm. on Interstate and Foreign Commerce, 85th Cong., 2d Sess., Report on the Television Inquiry: The Problem of Television Service for Smaller Communities 47 (Comm. Print 1958).

23. S. 2653, 86th Cong., 1st Sess. (1959).

24. S. 2653, sec. 330(b)(1)(2).

25. *See e.g.,* S. 1044 and H.R. 6840, 87th Cong., 1st Sess. (1961).

26. First Report and Order in Dockets 14895 and 15233, 38 F.C.C. 683 (1965).

27. Second Report and Order in Dockets 14895, 15233 and 15971, 2 F.C.C. 2d 725 (1966).

28. The first judicial consideration of the problem occurred in *Carter Mountain Transmission Corp. v. F.C.C.,* 321 F.2d 359 (D.C. Cir. 1963) (*see* chapter 4.)

29. *Back Mountain Telecable, Inc.,* Docket No. 16866, 5 F.C.C.2d 735 (1966).

30. *Id.* at 740.

31. *Id.*

32. 319 U.S. 190 (1943).

33. 321 F.2d 359 (D.C. Cir. 1963).

34. 352 F.2d 729 (D.C. Cir. 1965).

35. 5 F.C.C.2d at 740.

36. *Id.* at 742.

37. *Id.* at 743.

38. Memorandum Opinion and Order in Dockets 14895, 15223, and 15971, 6 F.C.C.2d 309 (1967).

39. *Id.* at 310.

40. *Id.*

41. *Id.* at 311.

42. *Id.* at 332.

43. *Id.* at 334.

44. *Id.* at 341.

45. *Id.*

46. 2 F.C.C.2d 725 at 787 (1966).

47. *Regulation of Community Antenna Television Systems: Hearings on H.R. 12914, H.R. 13286, and H.R. 14201 Before the House Comm. on Interstate and Foreign Commerce,* 89th Cong., 1st Sess. (1966).

48. *Id.* at 153.

49. H.R. Rep. No. 1635, 89th Cong., 2d Sess. 16 (1966).

50. *Id.* at 23.

51. *Id.* at 25.

52. Notice of Proposed Rulemaking and Notice of Inquiry in Docket 18397, 15 F.C.C.2d 417, 419–420 (1968).

53. Sloan Commission on Cable Communications, *On the Cable: The Television of Abundancje,* 92 (New York: McGraw Hill, 1971).

54. *F.C.C. Annual Report,* at 60 (1967).

55. *F.C.C. Annual Report,* at 46 (1968).

56. *Midwest Television, Inc.,* 13 F.C.C.2d 478 (1968).

57. *Id.* at 503.

58. *Id.* at 505.

59. Notice of Proposed Rulemaking, *supra* note 52.

60. First Report and Order in Docket 18397, 20 F.C.C.2d 201 (1969).

61. *Midwest Video v. U.S.,* 441 F.2d 1322 (8th Cir. 1971), *rev'd,* 406 U.S. 649 (1972).

62. First Report, *supra* note 60, at 205, *quoting, Associated Press v. United States,* 326 U.S. 1 at 20 (1945).

63. Cable Television Report and Order, 36 F.C.C.2d 143, 190–93 (1972).

64. *Id.* at 196 (1972) [although the ruling was later modified to trigger access channels on the basis of system size rather than market size, Report and Order in Docket 20508, 59 F.C.C.2d 294 (1976)].

65. First Report and Order, *supra* note 60, at 206.

66. *See* notes *infra.* 72, 78, 80.

67. 41 R.R.2d 361 (1977).

68. *Id.* at 364.

69. *Id.* at 365.

70. In re.: Cable Systems, Inc., 43 R.R.2d 665 (1978).

71. Those cases included, *Buckeye Cablevision, Inc. v. F.C.C.,* 387 F.2d 220 (D.C. Cir. 1967); *Black Hills Video Corp. v. F.C.C.,* 399 F.2d 65 (8th Cir. 1968), and *U.S. v. Southwestern Cable Co.,* 392 U.S. 157 (1968).

72. Cable Systems, Inc., *supra,* at 670.

73. *U.S. v. O'Brien*, 391 U.S. 367, 376–77 (1968).

74. Also interesting is the subsequent use of *O'Brien* by the Court of Appeals which came to a conclusion just the opposite of the commission's, *see*, chapter 4.

75. 43 R.R.2d 781 (1978).

76. *Home Box Office v. F.C.C.*, 567 F.2d 9 (D.C. Cir. 1977).

77. *See* disc. *infra.* chapter 4.

78. 43 R.R.2d at 790 n.14.

79. *See, e.g., Back Mountain, supra.*

80. Cable Systems, Inc., 45 R.R.2d 676 (1979); Video Vision, Inc., 45 R.R.2d 1136 (1979), and Dublin Associates, Ltd., 45 R.R.2d 1643 (1979).

81. 45 R.R.2d at 1645; 45 R.R.2d at 1141, and 45 R.R.2d at 667–68.

82. The rules were eliminated in 1980, 79 F.C.C.2d 663 (1980).

83. Report and Order in Docket 19988, 49 F.C.C.2d 1090 (1974).

84. Notice of Proposed Rulemaking in Docket 20363, 51 F.C.C.2d 519 (1975).

85. Report and Order in Docket 20363, 54 F.C.C.2d 207, 215 (1975).

86. Report and Order in Docket 20508, 59 F.C.C.2d 294, 296 (1976).

87. Staff of the House Comm. on Interstate and Foreign Commerce, Cable Television: Promise versus Regulatory Performance, 94th Cong. 2d Sess. (1976).

88. *Hearings on Cable Television Regulation Oversight Before the House Comm. on Interstate and Foreign Commerce,* 94th Cong., 2d Sess. (1976).

89. Option Papers, Committee on Interstate Commerce, Subcomm. on Communications, 95th Cong. 1st. Sess., (1977), at 541.

90. *See e.g.,* S. 622 (1979), S. 611 (979), S. 2827 (1980), and S. 898 (1981).

91. Sen. Barry Goldwater, chairman of the Senate Subcommittee on Communications, acting on a promise to municipal leaders, had sections of S. 898 dealing with cable deleted until he could hold hearings on comprehensive cable regulation. *See, Broadcasting,* 21 September 1981, at 25.

92. S. 2172, 98th Cong., 1st Sess. (1982).

93. Cable Communications Policy Act of 1984, Pub. L. No. 98-549.

94. *See generally, Cable Telecommunications Act of 1983: Hearings Before the Subcomm. on Communications of the Senate Comm. on Commerce, Science, and Transportation,* S. Hrg. 98-26, and *Options for Cable Legislation: Hearings Before the Sub comm. on Communications of the House Comm. on Energy and Commerce,* 98th Cong. 1st Sess, (1983) (Serial no. 98-73)

95. *See, e.g.,* testimony of New York City Mayor Ed Koch on behalf of the U.S. Conference of Mayors, *Options for Cable Legislation, id.* at 183–91.

96. *See e.g.,* testimony of Thomas Wheeler, President of the National Cable Television Association, *id.* at 28–63.

97. Cable Communications Act, sec. 602(6).

98. H.R. Rep. 98-934, 98th Cong. 2nd Sess. 31 (1984).

99. S. Rep. 98-67, 98th Cong. 2d Sess. 23 (1983).

100. *Id.* at 22.

4
The Courts Consider Cable

More than thirty-five years after the birth of CATV, there is still no clear-cut judicial position on the First Amendment standing of cable; no unified body of precedent exists which might guide those in industry and government, or clarify the relationship of the media to the citizenry. There does seem to be a modern trend in judicial thinking about cable TV, but this trend is by no means uniform.

To establish at least the beginning of a truly consistent policy requires a decision on the question from the Supreme Court, which is the final judge of all First Amendment issues and the body that gives practical shape and meaning to the Constitution. But until 1985, the Supreme Court had repeatedly declined to consider the question of cable's constitutional role. Further, the federal appellate courts—the judicial layer of authority directly beneath the Supreme Court—and the federal district courts beneath them, have failed to come to agreement on the issues. These lower courts have listened to arguments on both sides of the constitutional debate and have rendered some important decisions. Too frequently, however, the decision of one jurisdiction has been at odds with the decision of another, leaving cable with varying levels of constitutional protection around the country.

A close examination of the court's handling of the cable issue over the past twenty-five years reveals, as in the regulatory arena, three distinct stages in the treatment of the medium, which have been driven, once again, by the definition of cable TV.

Stage I: The Auxiliary Medium and the Courts

The first federal court case in which cable television was an issue appears to have been *Clarksburg Publishing Co. v. F.C.C.,* in 1955,[1] involving a challenge to the application for a broadcast license based on cross-ownership concerns. The applicant in question owned a cable system which, if it had been considered a regulated service, would have provided grounds for a cross-ownership complaint. Among the peripheral questions the court considered was whether cable could be classified as a service subject to FCC regulation. The commission had not yet asserted such jurisdiction and the question was an open one. The court concluded that the nature of cable was such that it could conceivably fall under FCC rules, even if such authority had not yet been invoked:

> The Commission will presumably assert jurisdiction to regulate community antenna systems if and when it concludes that such systems provide or are adjuncts of a broadcast service. Its failure thus far to assert such jurisdiction, standing by itself, cannot support a conclusion that the systems are not a service within the meaning of the rule.[2]

While the case did not deal directly with the First Amendment, the dicta does provide an early indication of how cable was perceived. The implication, again, is that CATV was some form of auxiliary broadcast service that could be federally controlled.

The possibility that some constitutional questions relevant to regulation might exist did not come before the courts until 1963, when the FCC first moved to take control of cable in *Carter Mountain*. Failing to win its argument at the FCC, the company went to the D.C. Circuit Court,[3] thereby beginning a process of litigation that provided the first major judicial statements on cable's constitutional standing. In its hearing before the D.C. Circuit, the microwave company argued that, among other things, the commission rules constituted an abridgment of First Amendment rights of the cable companies that received the microwave signals in question. The court, however, dismissed the First Amendment argument, pointing out that the rights of the cable systems were not at issue since the FCC rules restricted only the microwave operator and not the cable company directly. Further, the court explained that the FCC had complete constitutional authority, under *N.B.C. v. U.S.*[4] to regulate the airwaves:

> It may be assumed that any denial of a license to transmit radio or television programs keeps off the air, and hence deprives the public of, the material which the applicant desires to communicate. But that does not mean that the Commission must grant every license which is requested. Nor does it mean that the whole statutory system of regulation is invalid. Quite the contrary is true: a denial of a station license, validly made because the standard of "public interest, convenience and necessity" has not been met, is not a denial of free speech.[5]

Two years later the D.C. Circuit turned away a request that FCC rules on nonduplication of programming[6] be struck down. The plaintiffs in *Idaho Microwave, Inc. v. F.C.C.* argued, in part, that the rules violated the First

Amendment rights of the microwave company that imported the signals.[7] In contrast to *Carter Mountain,* the constitutional question was squarely before the bench in this case because the rules at issue did affect the normal operation of the cable system as well as that of the microwave relay company. But because the aggrieved party was still a microwave company, a service that used the airwaves, the rationale for upholding the rules remained the same: the need for regulation of a scarce, publicly owned resource.

The logic underlying these two decisions was persuasive if the foundation of *N.B.C. v. U.S.* was accepted. They were simple extensions of the broadcast doctrine and so perhaps unremarkable, for if the commission could regulate broadcasting it could regulate microwave companies. But how the cases were used later by the courts is of some interest.

The first CATV case in which substantive First Amendment questions were addressed by the court in a situation not involving microwave was *Buckeye Cablevision, Inc. v. F.C.C.* in 1967.[8] Following the commission's Second Report and Order in 1966, it ordered Buckeye Cablevision to halt the importation of distant television signals into Toledo, Ohio. Buckeye appealed the order, charging that, among other things, it violated the company's First Amendment right to freedom of speech. The court dismissed the proposition without significant written consideration, responding tersely that, "It is true that CATV disseminates programs carrying a wide range of information. But we think the restraint imposed by the rules is no more than is reasonably required to effectuate the public interest requirements of the [Federal Communications] Act."[9]

In fact, very little consideration was given the issue. More important than the court's conclusion, however, was its use of *N.B.C. v. U.S.* and *Carter Mountain* as precedent. Here, for the first time, the court extended case law based on the scarcity rationale to a situation that did not involve the airwaves. The facts of *Buckeye* were not analogous to *N.B.C., Carter Mountain,* or any other broadcast-bound medium, and the constitutional question probably should not have been dismissed so easily on those grounds.

What the decision demonstrated was the degree to which the courts, at this time, were bound up, as the regulatory agencies were, in a perception of cable television that could not be separated from broadcast television. In the crudest terms, television simply was, to many, television, whether it came over the airwaves or over a wire, and since very few systems did much more than retransmit broadcast signals, the technical distinction was not emphasized in the daily programming. Dicta from a 1968 case in the Fourth Circuit Court of Appeals is representative of the judicial viewpoint at this time:

> Appreciation of [the F.C.C.'s] problems is reflected in the history of CATV's origin, its development and its relation to television nationwide. It is primarily a televisionary [sic] complement. Further, a CATV system is very

largely dependent upon the existence of a live station, from which is obtained its stock in trade—TV programs.[10]

Cable television as an auxiliary service, an extension of television, was the dominant model in all regulatory spheres. So pervasive was this perception that even the Supreme Court adopted it as the framework within which to build early cable law. This phenomenon could be seen in one of the High Court's first CATV cases, *Fortnightly v. United Artists* in 1968. [11] The issue was cable's copyright liability, rather than the First Amendment, but it, nonetheless, illustrated the dominant perspective. Was cable a service that performed material and therefore liable for copyright? The court answered by declining to recognize CATV as a separate, independent communication system capable of initiating speech. Justice Potter Stewart, for the court, explained that both viewers and broadcasters had crucial roles within the framework of the television delivery system, and

> [w]hen CATV is considered in this framework, we conclude that it falls on the viewer's side of the line. Essentially, a CATV system no more than enhances the viewer's capacity to receive the broadcast signals; it provides a well-located antenna with an efficient connection to the viewer's set. . . . CATV equipment is powerful and sophisticated, but the basic function the equipment serves is little different from that served by the equipment generally furnished by a television viewer.[12]

Cable television, therefore, was not a medium and not a speaker in the First Amendment sense of the word. It was considered variously as either an extension of the viewer's antenna, an extension of the broadcast system, or simply a passive retransmission system with little or no discretion as to program content.

While the paradigm of the courts mirrored that of the FCC and Congress, it also trailed it by several years, and as Congress and the FCC moved into the era of cable as public resource, most courts still clung to the image of CATV as an ancillary service. A series of cases brought before three different circuit courts in 1968 were representative. In *Black Hills Video Corp. v. F.C.C.* in the Eighth Circuit,[13] *Conley Electronics Corp. v. F.C.C.* in the Tenth Circuit,[14] and *Titusville Cable TV, Inc. v. United States* in the Third Circuit,[15] various First Amendment attacks on government regulation were repelled. All the cases involved the FCC's 1966 Second Report and Order. *Black Hills* attacked the entire Report and Order, while *Conley* and *Titusville* addressed only the nonduplication rules. In each, however, the courts upheld the constitutionality of the rules using as precedent prior cases based, in part, on the scarcity rationale. In *Conley,* for example, the Tenth Circuit noted, "Several courts have rejected similar contentions in upholding a denial by the Commission of a license by a microwave carrier seeking to serve a CATV system," and microwave cases were "indistinguishable" from the pure cable case at hand. "In both situations what is involved is reasonable regulation in the public interest," the Tenth Circuit continued, citing *N.B.C., Carter Mountain,* and *Buckeye.*[16]

And when the cable operators argued that the scarcity rationale was inapplicable, the court retreated to the justification of an inseparable relationship between broadcasting and CATV. Said the court in *Black Hills:*

> The Commission's effort to preserve local television by regulating CATV has the same constitutional status under the First Amendment as regulation of the transmission of signals by the originating television stations. It is irrelevant to the congressional power that the CATV systems do not themselves use the airwaves in their distribution systems. The crucial consideration is that they do use radio signals and that they have a unique impact upon and relationship with the television broadcast service.[17]

Such perceptions go far in explaining why there was no consideration of the First Amendment in the first challenge to the commission's authority to reach the Supreme Court. In a decision handed down just a few days before *Fortnightly,* the only question that concerned the justices was that of commission authority under the Communications Act. In the landmark *United States v. Southwestern Cable Co.* in 1968, [18] the Court dwelt only upon the statutory parameters of FCC jurisdiction, concluding that cable constituted "interstate communication by wire" as per Section 152(a) of the Communications Act and was, therefore, generally subject to FCC regulation for the purposes of advancing the orderly development of the television system in the United States. The limits of that authority were left ill-defined, with the only guidance in the admonition that such regulations be "reasonably ancillary" to the commission regulation of broadcasting, implying that jurisdiction did not extend to cable in all situations.[19] But nowhere in the decision did the court discuss possible constitutional problems. The words "freedom of speech" do not appear in any of the opinions.

By 1969 it was possible for the courts, leaning on a solid body of law, to dismiss quickly any claim of First Amendment rights for cable operators or cable viewers. *Total Telecable v. F.C.C.,* a 1969 case that, in part, challenged the constitutionality of specific FCC nonduplication regulations, was typical. Said the Ninth Circuit:

> Total argues that the non-duplication rule is invalid because it is an improper restraint on free speech in violation of the First Amendment. This argument has been considered and rejected in a number of cases, and we agree with them. (Citing, *Titusville, Black Hills, Conley* and *Buckeye.*)[20]

This model of CATV as a passive reception-retransmission service re-mained the major perspective at the Supreme Court and in many appellate courts well into the 1970s, long after Congress and the FCC had accepted a new model grounded in the concept of cable as an independent and active component in the national communications system.

Stage II: The Search for Direction

Greater Freemont: Precursor to Doubt

The passive model of cable television was pervasive in the late 1960s, but not monolithic. In the regulatory and public sectors, as has been pointed out, the model already had turned to one of a public information utility. This vision was still years away in the courts, but at least one jurisdiction in 1968 challenged the accepted model and suggested that the First Amend-ment could play an important role in the formulation of cable regulation. In doing so, it presaged court decisions of nearly a decade later.

The case was *Greater Freemont, Inc. v. City of Freemont* in 1968.[21] A federal district court in Ohio found that when a cable company contracted with the local telephone company to do the actual stringing and maintenance of wires, the cable operator could not be regulated under a city franchise ordinance. The court reasoned that the franchise could be based only on the use of public streets, alleys, and so forth, and the cable company did not directly use these public thoroughfares. While this case did not turn on the First Amendment question, the court did note in dicta that there was no major conceptual difference between CATV and "newspapers, television, radio, books and magazines" in that all delivered news and information: "When we consider CATV in this role, we are approaching the areas of freedom of speech and the press protected by the First Amendment."[22]

The court then evoked the equal protection clause of the Fourteenth Amendment, explaining that controls similar to the one at issue for cable could not be applied to other media.

The language of this decision suggested, for one of the first times in court history, the removal of cable from its classification as a simple conduit. Instead, CATV was seen as a communications system conceptually similar to other media. Naturally, such an elevation in definitional status brought with it concurrent protection under the First Amendment. The court failed to make the important constitutional distinction between the variable rights of different media (i.e., broadcast versus print) and so provided no grounding for the form that cable rights might take, but the case still suggested a small break from the mainstream judicial perception of cable at the time.

Evolution of the Model

This early skepticism might be cited as a starting point in the confusion and disagreement about cable that marked the 1970s. Rulings in the early and mid-1970s harbingered a general breakdown in the retransmission model by taking a more critical look at the applicability of precedent grounded in the scarcity doctrine. This, in turn, led some courts in the late 1970s to an outright rejection of all rationales for cable regulation and eventual acceptance of a First Amendment shield for the medium. At the same time, other courts moved instead toward a broadcast formula for cable regulation, suggesting a continued need for control and promoting varying rationales for the constitutional legitimation of such control.

Part of the early confusion stemmed from the medium's dual potential for program origination and program retransmission. The courts began to accept the editorial function associated with production but had difficulty in transferring that function (and the legal controls it implied) to the retransmission service. This was seen quite clearly in two important Supreme Court cases of the early 1970s, *United States v. Midwest Video Corp.* in 1972[23] and *Teleprompter v. C.B.S.* in 1974.[24]

The former sprang from a challenge by Midwest Video Corporation to the FCC's 1969 order mandating local origination. In deciding the case, the appellate court drew from the Supreme Court's opinion in *Fortnightly,* explaining that cable was simply an extension of the viewer's antenna and could not be turned into a broadcasting service solely because the FCC thought it was a good idea.[25] While the court did concede that cable was a "new and distinct form of electronic communication," it remained a system that "no more than enhances the viewer's capacity to receive broadcast signals."[26]

On appeal, however, the Supreme Court reversed the ruling and upheld the FCC's regulations. The majority concluded the commission did have the statutory authority to impose the rules. By doing so, though, the court not only seemed to contradict its previous conceptual position and acknowledge cable as an information producer, it forced the medium into that role. Cable was swiftly and, in this case, most reluctantly, elevated to the level of an information provider. The minority opinion, led by Justice William O. Douglas, maintained the more established doctrine, arguing that cable was not a broadcasting service and could not be turned into one at the whim of the FCC.

By itself the case seemed to suggest a possible change of vision, but in contrast with *Teleprompter* two years later, it appeared to speak to a confusion about the evolving nature of the medium. In *Teleprompter* the court was asked to reconsider its ruling in *Fortnightly,* specifically on the grounds that a fundamental change had taken place in the nature of cable television. The plaintiffs argued that cable was now taking an active part in the selection, alteration, and redistribution of television signals and, therefore, ought to be held liable, at least in some circumstances, for copyright infringement.

The appeals court was partially sympathetic to the plea and constructed a formula for compromise in which copyright would apply only to signals imported from distant towns and which viewers could not normally receive. Copyright would not apply to retransmitted signals viewers could get without the aid of CATV.[27]

The Supreme Court, however, rejected the appellate court's innovative solution, steadfastly maintaining the position taken in *Fortnightly*. Stated Justice Stewart, for the majority, "The reception and rechanneling of these [TV] signals for simultaneous viewing is essentially a viewer function."[28] He denied the possibility that cable operators exercised any broad choice in the programs they selected and carried, stating that broadcasters maintained a wide latitude in choosing programs, but CATV only picked up one signal from the airwaves, at which time its editorial freedom was extinguished.[29] The majority decision appeared to conflict with the notion of cable as a message producer, a role which the court had mandated for cable in *Midwest Video I* two years before.

Meanwhile, the minority opinion in *Teleprompter* suggested the beginning of a new viewpoint. Justice Douglas, joined by Chief Justice Burger, argued—in concert with the plaintiffs—that there had been an important change in the medium. Unlike the cable systems involved in *Fortnightly,* "present CATV's are functionally equivalent to a regular broadcaster," said the Chief Justice.[30]

Taken together, the cases pointed out the problems the judiciary had in dealing with cable once the passive retransmission model was even partially abandoned. Embedded in this difficulty was the compounding question about the role of scarcity. The courts in the early and mid-1960s had applied the scarcity doctrine to cable without a great deal of analysis and, when challenged on the point, retreated to a position that implied the issue was not necessarily relevant in any case.

As the courts of the 1970s began rethinking the role of cable, the question of scarcity arose again. This time, the courts were much more cautious in their treatment of the issue. One example was a 1969 case called *Great Falls Community TV Cable Co. v. F.C.C.*, in which a cable company challenged FCC nonduplication rules by arguing that content regulation of cable was unconstitutional without a showing of scarcity.[31] It called as precedent upon the recently decided *Red Lion Broadcasting* case,[32] which upheld the Fairness Doctrine on scarcity grounds. In its decision, the court implicitly admitted that the scarcity rationale did not apply to cablecasters, but it nonetheless confirmed the authority of the FCC.

In our view, nothing in *Red Lion* impairs the authority of [previous decisions on this point]. Although it is true that the *Red Lion* opinion proceeded from the scarcity-frequency premise, the court expressly declined to reach arguments justifying the doctrine on other, independent grounds.[33]

In other words, even though scarcity may not be present, other factors might exist sufficient to justify regulation. The rationale that the court eventually adopted was that of the supremacy of the First Amendment rights of the public and the FCC's role in guarding those rights, but at no time did the court admit that there might be CATV operator rights at stake as well.

Subsequently, in *Midwest Video I* in 1972, the Supreme Court joined in the abandonment of the scarcity doctrine for cable, advancing a substitute rationale for regulation similar to that of the appeals court in *Great Falls*. The substitute took the initial form of the commission's authority to promulgate regulations reasonably ancillary to its oversight in broadcasting. This statutory rationale was further grounded in the implicit constitutional responsibility of the FCC to promote diversified programming, and was, thus, supported by the general precedent of *Red Lion* rather than hurt by it. Explained Justice Brennan for the court:

> To be sure, the cablecasts required may be transmitted without the use of the broadcast spectrum. But that regulation is not the less, for that reason, reasonably ancillary to the Commission's jurisdiction over broadcast services. The effect of the regulation, after all, is to assure that in the retransmission of broadcast signals, the viewers are provided suitable diversified programming, the same objective underlying regulation sustained in *N.B.C. v. U.S.*[34]

Scarcity, therefore, might not be applicable to cable, but other rationales existed to serve as the foundation for regulation. These included the doctrine of ancillarity and the superior First Amendment right of the people as explicated in the broadcast cases.

There were potential problems in this position, however. In the first place, a question existed as to how far the ancillarity doctrine stretched. Was it sufficient, in and of itself, to overcome arguable cablecaster First Amendment rights? Coupled with the First Amendment right of the people it might provide a persuasive argument, but there were problems with the combination as well. Under *Red Lion* the supremacy of the people's right was inextricably intertwined with the scarcity argument. Without scarcity, the broadcast equation had to be reversed; the right of the individual communicator had to take precedence over the right of the people to a free flow of information. Therefore, by denying a scarcity argument in cable, the courts were endangering the regulatory rationale based on service to the community.

All these related problems represented significant cracks in the façade of court precedent that had been erected in the late 1960s and early 1970s. In the late 1970s and early 1980s, these cracks began to widen, and eventually the construction crumbled. An important juncture in this process was the appellate court decision in *Home Box Office v. F.C.C.* in 1977.[35]

Home Box Office was the first major case dealing with FCC cable rules to come to the federal courts after *Midwest Video I,* and it marked a critical turning point in the evolution of cable rights. At issue were FCC rules governing and limiting the programming that cablecasters could offer on a pay basis.[36] Under the rules, operators were prohibited from offering, on a subscriber basis, certain movies and sporting events. The commission and competing broadcasters claimed such programming could potentially siphon similar fare away from free television and into subscriber cable services and that such competition was not in the public interest.

The D.C. Circuit Court held against the FCC and struck down the prohibitions. It found that the regulations went beyond the FCC's statutory jurisdiction, and it concluded that the rules violated the First Amendment rights of cablecasters.[37] The significance of the decision for present purposes was that it marked the first major application of First Amendment protection to cable. In extending this protection, the court took time to reevaluate the propriety of applying the scarcity doctrine to cable regulation. As noted, previous courts admitted the absence of scarcity, but always seemed to find alternative justification for regulation. The D.C. Circuit could not, stating flatly:

> The First Amendment theory espoused in *National Broadcasting Co.* and reaffirmed in *Red Lion Broadcasting* cannot be directly applied to cable television since an essential precondition of that theory—physical interference and scarcity requiring an umpiring role for government—is absent.[38]

The court went on, in footnote, to criticize earlier cable decisions in which scarcity, directly or indirectly, was called upon as a rationale for regulation. According to the court, such previous decisions were clearly the result of faulty logic. It was noted, for example, that in *Buckeye Cablevision,* "the court, without discussion, cited *National Broadcasting Co.* and *Carter Mountain,* thus apparently incorrectly treating the case as one involving the scarcity and allocation rationale."[39] Cases such as *Buckeye* and *Black Hills* could not, it explained, be validly used to support the proposition that the regulations at issue were constitutional as extensions of the justifiable rules used in the regulation of broadcasting.

The court then addressed an issue that would become central in the debate over cable rights, the question of economic scarcity: Was there a scarcity of media voices, or system owners, in a given area that had been brought about not by technological constraints but rather by industry economics, and more importantly, was the existence of such a monopoly situation adequate grounds for government intervention in an otherwise constitutionally protected industry? In the newspaper business, economic forces had created the common situation of one-newspaper towns, one editorial voice per community. Many argued that cable companies were inherently economic monopolies, that more than one could not operate profitably in a given area.

The long-standing policy of the courts was that technical scarcity—scarcity created by a limited physical spectrum—was sufficient grounds to justify state control of broadcasting. But what of economic scarcity? In a landmark 1974 case, the Supreme Court rejected the argument that, for newspapers at least, economic scarcity could serve the same purpose. In *Miami Herald Publishing Co. v. Tornillo,* the court declared that economic scarcity was not grounds for an open access requirement for newspapers.[40] The ramifications of this decision for cable became apparent in the decision of the appeals court in *Home Box Office.*

Home Box Office represented the fruition of a judicial perspective of cable television as an independent medium of communication rather than an adjunct of an already established media form, and pulled cable away from over-the-air TV in a dramatic way by stating that it was more closely analogous to the print medium. The court pointed out that, even if an argument could be made that cable was economically, rather than technically, a scarce resource, such a showing could not be sufficient to establish grounds for the kind of regulations imposed by the FCC. The court stated:

> In any case, scarcity which is solely of economic conditions is apparently insufficient to justify even limited government intrusion into the First Amendment rights of the conventional press (see, *Miami Herald Publishing Co. v. Tornillo*) and there is nothing in the record before us to suggest a constitutional distinction between cable television and newspapers on this point.[41]

In this passage, the court elevated CATV out of its twenty-five year status as an auxiliary service. It appeared to give cable First Amendment standing equal to that of the print media. In fact, the test finally used by the court to determine the legitimacy of governmental intervention here was drawn from the symbolic speech case, *United States v. O'Brien,* mentioned in chapter 3.[42]

As noted there, even in the case of pure speech, which is granted the highest standard of First Amendment protection, some government intervention is occasionally justified by a compelling state interest. Such intervention is permissible, however, only when the regulations in question "further an important or substantial government interest; . . . and if the incidental restriction on alleged First Amendment freedoms is no greater than is essential to the furtherance of that interest."[43]

In *Home Box Office,* the court held that the FCC regulations fell far short of the mark on both counts and, accordingly, found the rules in violation of the Constitution. Unfortunately, the new approach was neither confirmed nor denied by a Supreme Court opinion, for the court declined to review the case.

The Supreme Court did agree to hear an important subsequent case, however, *F.C.C. v. Midwest Video Corp. (Midwest Video II)*, two years later in 1979.[44] Although the High Court's decision there avoided the First Amendment question, the case was significant for a variety of reasons, not the least of which was that it marked the court's first movement to strike down any FCC cable regulation. The case sprang from the commission's 1976 requirements on public and leased access channels.[45] Midwest Video Corp. challenged the rules as beyond the commission's statutory authority and as unconstitutional abridgments of expression.

A strongly worded decision at the appellate level found in favor of the cable company and took a position that cable had significant First Amendment interests.[46] The Eighth Circuit stated bluntly:

> The Commission does not favor us with any views as to: (1) why cable systems are not entitled to the same First Amendment rights as other private media, such as newspapers and movie theaters; (2) how compelled access to cable facilities is distinguishable, in a First Amendment context, from compelled access to broadcast facilities; or (3) how its rule . . . requiring cable operators to exercise prior restraint in obscenity, and exposure of cable owners to lawsuits resulting from its access rules, can be justified.[47]

The court discussed cable in terms of electronic publications and found the FCC rules comparable to government attempts to force newspapers to devote editorial pages to whomever wished to have them.[48] It examined possible rationales for interfering in a cable operator's First Amendment rights—considering then quickly rejecting scarcity—and focused most of its attention on the FCC contention that the rules served the broader First Amendment interests of the people in promoting a diversity of viewpoints. In weighing the asserted rights of the public against those of the cable owners, the court found the former wanting. The court declared that the rights of cable operators arose from the Constitution; the public's right "to get on television" stemmed from the "Commission's desire to create that right."[49] As laudable as the FCC's goals may be, said the court, "we deal here with the Federal Communications Commission, not the Federal First Amendment Commission."[50]

Ultimately, the court invoked a kind of "clear and present danger" test to determine the legitimacy of government intrusion as represented by the commission's rules.[51] The regulations, unsurprisingly, failed to meet the stringent criteria of the test.

As in *Home Box Office* the constitutional test applied to cable was one traditionally reserved for the stronger protection afforded pure speech cases, rather than the lesser tests associated with unprotected communication.

The appellate decision lacked the constitutional importance of strong precedent due to the court's option to resolve the question on statutory grounds. Nonetheless, it noted: "Were it necessary to decide the issue, the present record would render the intrusion represented by the present rules constitutionally impermissible."[52]

On appeal, the Supreme Court upheld the lower court's decision and, in the process, at last conceded that cable had some characteristics of an independent mode of mass communication. Without recalling its earlier pronouncement that cable operators lacked any significant degree of editorial control over their product, the court observed that CATV had advanced to a point where such control was common. Stated the majority:

> Cable operators now share with broadcasters a significant amount of editorial discretion regarding what their programming will include. As the Commission itself has observed, "both in their signal carriage decisions and in connection with their origination function, cable television systems are afforded considerable control over the content of the programming they provide."[53]

The court compared cable to broadcasting in several respects but declined to draw any parallels between cable and the print media, as had the lower court. It raised cable to a position of legal protection equivalent to that of broadcaster, but would go no further. The limits of FCC jurisdiction over broadcast television, held the court, defined the limits of its jurisdiction over cable. Basing much of its thinking on the ancillarity doctrine, the court drew heavily from its decision in *C.B.S. v. D.N.C.*, in which a plea for mandatory forced access to broadcast channels was rejected on the grounds that such access amounted to turning broadcasters into common carriers.[54] The regulations were, thus, rejected on statutory grounds, and the court never reached the more important question of First Amendment status raised by the lower court.[55]

H.B.O. and *Midwest Video II* helped establish the legitimacy of a new perspective on cable's constitutional position. Together, the cases provided a foundation for the legal argument that cable ought to have First Amendment rights parallel to those of newspapers, and they cast increasing doubt on the equation that linked cable's rights to those of broadcasting.

While these cases can be considered the starting point in the growth of a stronger constitutional role for cable, they were starting points only and did not represent a judicial consensus. As case law moved through the mid-1980s, this print protection model of cable appeared to be claiming growing numbers of judicial adherents, but at the time of the *Midwest Video II* decision, such a trend was not at all in evidence. There did appear to be a measure of agreement on the nature of the technology. It was no longer thought of simply as an ancillary service; it was a new and distinct medium, but its constitutional nature was still very much uncertain. Two appeals courts placed it on an equal footing with print. The Supreme Court, while not facing the question directly, implied a First Amendment parity with broadcasting, and the argument that cable could and should be controlled for the benefit of the community was forcefully enunciated in two cases in the early 1980s that provided a strong counterpoint to *H.B.O.* and *Midwest Video II.* These were *Community Communications Co. v. Boulder*[56] and *Berkshire Cablevision v. Burke.*[57]

The Print Model Challenged

The rather involved facts of *C.C.C. v. Boulder* centered on an attempt by the city of Boulder, Colorado to prevent a franchise, Community Communications Co. (CCC), from expanding beyond the specific neighborhood which it had for some years been serving. Local officials, after long debate, had decided to revoke the company's original franchise, which had given CCC the right to wire the entire city, and replace it with a franchise that restricted the company to one particular neighborhood. In a series of legal actions in federal court, the company challenged the city's move as a violation of both federal antitrust laws and the First Amendment. While final disposition of the case rested only upon the antitrust question, the First Amendment issues were given extensive consideration at both the district and appellate court levels.

The cable company argued that Boulder's attempt to prevent it from expanding its service area represented an unlawful prior restraint on its right to communicate. It claimed that comparable prohibitions on newspapers would be struck down as unconstitutional and, for purposes of the case at hand, no difference existed between cable and print. The city responded by declaring the newspaper analogy inappropriate and claiming that cable was a natural monopoly. Therefore, said the city, some reasonable governmental control did not offend the Constitution.

The federal district court and Appellate Judge Markey (dissenting in the first of two appellate decisions) sided with the company.[58] While only a dissenting opinion, Judge Markey's position is important for it represented one side of the debate as well as the initial decision of the district court. The judge first concluded that cable was constitutionally protected in the same manner as newspapers, declaring:

> When, as studies show, the majority of our people get their news from television, I cannot, in First Amendment jurisprudence, and concerning ac-

tion to still a growing voice, distinguish the dissemination of news and information by cable TV from that by newspapers.[59]

He also argued that the city's actions violated not only the rights of the cable operator to speak, but also the right of the public to listen. Said the judge:

> In effect . . . the city has said to CCC, "Thou shall not speak your truth to any Boulder citizens residing outside your present area of operations for 90 days." To Boulder citizens in those areas, the city has said, "Thou shall not for 90 days hear CCC's speech." It is difficult to imagine a more flagrant and chilling inroad on cherished First Amendment freedoms.[60]

More importantly, Markey and the district court attacked the city's proposition that cable was a natural monopoly and, therefore, regulation was permissible. They first questioned the existence of technical scarcity. "Not to put too fine a point on it," stated Markey, "that argument is today simply fallacious."[61] The district court found, and Markey agreed, that at least four competing companies could be comfortably accommodated without adversely affecting public thoroughfares.[62] And, underscoring the analogy to newspapers, Markey drew on *Tornillo* to argue that even if economic scarcity existed in this context it was not sufficient reason to ignore the First Amendment interests of the cable company.[63] He stated that economic scarcity did not support government intrusion into First Amendment rights. The conclusion, then, was that there was no justification for the city's attempt to regulate cable in this manner.

In reversing the district court, the Tenth Circuit majority implied that the arguments of the company, Judge Markey, and the lower court were simplistic and failed to take into account obvious differences between the print medium and cable. According to Judge Seymour, writing for the court, the newspaper analogy did not stand up under close inspection:

> [I]t was inappropriate for the district court to summarily apply to cable operators the First Amendment principles governing newspapers. The nature and degree of protection afforded to First Amendment expressions in any given medium depends on that medium's particular characteristics.[64]

According to the court, cable, unlike newspapers, must create a significant disruption, in the form of stringing wire either on poles or underground, in order to deliver its message. Local governments must be permitted to regulate such public inconveniences.

More importantly, the court accepted the proposition that scarcity, at least economic scarcity, was insufficient justification for state intrusion into an otherwise protected area of expression. Specifically, the court held that the application of the *Miami Herald* case was misplaced due to the qualitative differences in the types of relationships between cities and newspapers, and cities and cable companies. The court argued that the *Miami Herald* case involved an effort by the state to compel access to a medium "that is not tied to government in the way that cable companies necessarily are."[65] In the cable industry, explained the court:

> There is no tradition of nearly absolute freedom from government control. Most importantly, a cable company must significantly impact the public domain in order to operate; without a license it cannot engage in cable broadcasting to disseminate information.[66]

Further, the court suggested that varying degrees of scarcity or monopoly, whatever the cause, might support varying degrees of government oversight:

> For example, differences in (1) the degree of natural monopoly or scarcity characterizing the medium, (2) the pace and potential for technological change, or (3) the uses and possible uses of the medium such as two-way cable communications, even interconnection, might make kinds of regulations constitutionally permissible in one medium that would be forbidden in another.[67]

In short, the majority in C.C.C. accepted cable as a new form of mass communication, but paused before inserting it into a framework of constitutional rights fashioned for an older medium. It suggested the existence of rationales for the legitimate regulation of cable and explored the character and nature of some of those rationales.

These threads of thought were picked up by the federal district court in Rhode Island a year later in *Berkshire Cablevision v. Burke*. While the arguments of the court were more sophisticated and powerful than those of the majority in C.C.C., the theme was similar: that the inherent technological differences between cable and print generate different economic, social, and constitutional realities.

The facts of the case involved Rhode Island regulations requiring mandated public access channels, the same issue that confronted the courts in *Midwest Video II*. But whereas the appeals court in *Midwest* concluded, in dicta, that such control violated the constitution, the court in *Burke* found the rules to be acceptable and even vital to the maintenance of First Amendment rights.

Berkshire challenged the state Public Utilities Commission (PUC) regulations requiring at least three access channels. The company claimed the rules abridged its First Amendment protection and, paralleling *Midwest Video II*, the company also challenged the PUC's statutory authority to promulgate the rules. Unlike *Midwest Video II*, the district court rejected the second argument without lengthy comment, finding the rules well within the PUC's power. As a result, the court was able to determine the constitutional question directly, unlike the situation in *Midwest*.

The judge carefully outlined the controversy over the appropriate model of First Amendment rights for cable, comparing *Red Lion* and *C.B.S. v. D.N.C.* (the broadcast model) with *Tornillo* (the print model), and concluding with a summary of the decision in *Midwest*. Observing the Eighth Circuit's finding that cable fell into the newspaper mold and ought to be afforded the same rights, the District Judge politely demurred:

> With all due deference to the Eighth and District of Columbia Circuits, I respectfully disagree with their analysis of the constitutionality of the access requirements for cable television systems. Newspapers and cable television cannot be equated. More to the point, they are constitutionally distinguishable.[68]

The judge found that distinction in three areas. The first was the historic nexus between cable and government and the contrary relationship between print and government. The second distinction was in cable's necessary use of public thoroughfares which opened the way for municipal oversight. The third was in cable's claimed economic scarcity.[69] The judge concluded that economic scarcity did exist in cable and was a sufficient reason for upholding access channels. The details of the judge's reasoning will be discussed later for they address a different approach to considering the relationship of the *Tornillo* decision to cable. For the moment it is sufficient to note the court's basic philosophical rationale:

> For this court at least, scarcity is scarcity—its particular source, whether "physical" or "economic" does not matter if its effect is to remove from all but a small group an important means of expressing ideas.[70]

The access rules were, therefore, constitutional. The legal weight of the decision was lost five years later when the appellate courts, citing exogenous circumstances, ruled the issue moot, but the logic of the decision is important and serves a comparative purpose here.

In *Berkshire v. Burke,* the Rhode Island Court enunciated a framework of cable rights that fell at one end of the philosophical spectrum. The decision of the appeals court in *H.B.O.* represented the other end. Both agreed that cable was different from television and, so, deserved a distinct constitutional treatment. This helped move the discussion out of the stagnant model of the 1960s, but it also generated new confusion about what cable's role ought to be. The search for a direction split along two divergent paths. The late 1960s and 1970s, therefore, can be seen as a time of transition in the legal environment of the medium, but also as a time of at least moderate constitutional confusion.

Stage III: The Beginning of Consensus(?)

With a series of cases beginning in 1982, some of the confusion seemed to be abating. This is not to suggest that a new and uniform approach to cable rights was suddenly coming into vogue. Important differences of opinion were still apparent among jurisdictions (and change does not occur quickly in matters of constitutional law). Nonetheless, the major cases dealing with cable and the First Amendment did seem to share a common theme, and so one could cautiously suggest the beginning of a new trend.

This trend rejected the logic of *C.C.C. v. Boulder* and *Burke,* and increasingly presented to cable greater portions of First Amendment protection. In the areas of local control over content, FCC regulation of signal carriage, and the franchising process itself, the courts struck down government regulations as a violation of the cablecaster's First Amendment rights.

The first in the new progression of cases dealt with government attempts to control obscene and indecent cable programming. In *Box Office v. Wilkinson* in 1982, a coalition of cable operators sought an injunction against enforcement of a Utah statute enacted to prohibit the cablecasting of obscene and indecent programs.[71] The law made it a crime to disseminate over cable not only legally obscene material but also programming that included nudity in nearly any context.

At least two lines of reasoning were available to the federal district court that heard the case. In the first instance, it could have followed the early view of cable which linked it with broadcast television for constitutional purposes. Under federal law, the airing of indecent material by broadcasters is prohibited,[72] and in *F.C.C. v. Pacifica Foundation*[73] in 1978, the Supreme Court upheld the FCC's authority to regulate the time and manner in which indecent, rather than obscene, speech could be presented by broadcasters. One of the main arguments of the government in that case was the alleged availability of the material to minors. The same argument was used by Utah in *Wilkinson* in the state's attempt to defend the statute against charges of unconstitutionality.[74]

The court could have also followed the precedent laid down in obscenity law as it has traditionally been applied to print and speech. The current standards here are outlined in *Miller v. California*[75] under which the mere presence of nudity or even sexual intercourse is insufficient in itself to brand a work obscene. Further, this view could call upon the Supreme Court's 1957 decision in *Butler v. Michigan* to rebut the contention that the standards for adult reading should be based on a consideration of what is appropriate for children.[76]

The district court followed the latter path, using an approach grounded in print and speech cases and applying the standards of *Miller* and *Butler* rather than those of *Pacifica* to find the Utah law in violation of the free speech rights of the cablecasters.

The decision was underscored in a similar case brought before the same court a short time later. In *Community Television of Utah v. Roy City*, the city of Roy, Utah passed an ordinance banning obscene and indecent material on cable, an ordinance the court again struck down as unconstitutional.[77]

Subsequently, a 1983 decision in Miami, Florida suggested that all municipal attempts to control indecent programming on cable would be doomed to a finding of unconstitutionality. In striking down the Miami ordinance in *Cruz v. Ferre*, the federal district court ruled that cable and broadcast TV were quite different media.[78] According to the court, the viewer, through his or her ability to monitor program guides, to decline overall service or specific shows, and to technically prevent children from viewing certain channels, was in much greater control of cable than broadcasting. "This opportunity to completely avoid the potential harm to minor or immature viewers sounds the death knell of *Pacifica's* applicability in the cable television context," stated the court.[79] This decision was upheld at the appellate level in 1985, with the appeals court using the same logic and much of the same language in its ruling.[80]

A similar constitutional perspective was used by the D.C. Circuit Court in 1985 when it struck down long-standing FCC rules that required cable operators to carry all the stations operating in or near their market.[81] According to these regulations, if a TV station could be received over the air by a home antenna, the cable system had to keep it on the system. The cable operators complained that these "must carry" rules often created redundancy in programming, that is, two stations carrying the same programs, and on systems with limited capacity, resulted in displacement of programming that was more specialized or in greater demand.

The ruling of the circuit court in this case, *Quincy Cable Television v. F.C.C.*, was not surprising since it came from the same court that handed down the decision proclaiming federal cable guidelines unconstitutional in the *H.B.O.* case. As in that case, the court first attacked the scarcity doctrine, noting that, "as this and other courts have recognized, the 'scarcity rationale' has no place in evaluating the government regulation of cable."[82]

Additionally, the D.C. Circuit rejected the argument that economic monopoly was a sufficient basis for the FCC rules. It repeated its position in *H.B.O.* that economic scarcity alone could not justify government intrusion into presumed First Amendment rights (again citing *Tornillo*). But the court also went further, for the first time suggesting that the assumption of economic scarcity itself in cable television might be without substantial foundation. Said the court, "the 'economic scarcity' argument rests on the entirely unproven—and indeed doubtful—assumption that cable operators are in a position to exact monopolistic charges."[83]

Finally, in response to the dicta in C.C.C., the court concluded that cable's use of the public rights of way did not provide the substantial justification necessary to maintain control over the content of the medium.[84]

In *Quincy*, then, a number of rationales historically used to justify government control of cable were addressed and found insufficient. While the case dealt with only one form of regulation, the logic permeated the framework of FCC authority over cable. Extending the argument of the court in *Quincy*, one could call into question much of the Cable Communications Act of 1984 itself. It seemed possible after the case that if a challenge to the act arose within the jurisdiction of the D.C. Circuit, that body would have little hesitation in finding the new law, or parts of it, unconstitutional.

In fact, a different jurisdiction had done nearly that only a few months before the *Quincy* decision. *Preferred Communications, Inc. v. Los Angeles* was potentially the most far-reaching decision of the mid-1980s, for it struck at the heart of the Cable Act.[85] A keystone of that legislation was its grant to cities of the right to issue franchises. This, in turn, provided the cities with their primary means of controlling cable development and service, and levying franchise fees (although, as previously noted, the legislation was a mixed bag and restricted cities as much as it legitimized their control).

The Eleventh Circuit Court in San Francisco held this key clause to be potentially unconstitutional.[86] The qualifier must be used because the court stopped just short of proclaiming the provision to be an outright violation of the First Amendment. But the court very explicitly held the city of Los Angeles' franchising system, which was typical of all franchising systems, to act as an unconstitutional prior restraint on the rights of expression of the cable company.

The case grew out of an attempt by a maverick cable company to set up a system in the south central area of Los Angeles without acquiring a permit from the city. Requests by the company for pole space to string wires had been rebuffed by local utility companies. The utilities told Preferred it would first have to obtain a city permit. The company was reluctant to enter into the very expensive process of winning the city franchise and instead challenged the entire franchising procedure in court. The federal district dismissed Preferred's claims, but the appeals court found the company's constitutional arguments to be persuasive.

Echoing a growing number of procable rulings, the Eleventh Circuit rejected what had become the major constitutional rationales for cable regulation: physical scarcity, economic scarcity, and disruption of public thoroughfares.

It declined to address directly the question of whether cable was a natural monopoly, noting that the decision in *Tornillo* had made the issue irrelevant.[87] The court said that cable's use of public and private rights of way justified some city control over construction and maintenance of the system, but such control did not extend to matters of content.[88]

Finally, the Eleventh Circuit considered the question of physical scarcity. In other regulatory contexts, previous jurisdictions had simply dismissed scarcity of frequency arguments, pointing out the inapplicability of the doctrine to the wire-bound medium. This case dealt with city franchising authority, however, and so raised the issue of scarcity of space on poles, rather than scarcity of channels, as grounds for regulation. Like the minority in C.C.C., the court found there to be sufficient space on the poles for an unspecified number of cable systems. Scarcity in this dimension, therefore, could not underpin regulation. Beyond this issue, however, the court concluded that the First Amendment compelled the government to grant access to pole space as long as there was room. The court determined that for cable companies, utility poles could be considered public forums. Just as citizens have a right to use city parks and town squares for protected, expressive activity, cable companies have special constitutional rights of access to the poles.[89] The use of both parks and the poles is subject to some reasonable amount of government regulation, but within these closely defined limits, must be kept open.

The court concluded that as long as there was space on the poles, the city was obligated under the First Amendment to provide access to all cable companies. A weakness of the decision was the court's avoidance of the question about what the city could do if space on the poles ran out, but the strong overriding statement was that cable enjoyed substantial First Amendment protection in its communicative activities.

Preferred, in fact, turned the Constitution against the cities and, potentially, against the Cable Communications Act. It raised the possibility that, like a stray thread, the decision could be continually tugged on in subsequent litigation until the broad fabric of cable regulation at the local, state, and federal levels began to completely unravel.

In June 1986, the Supreme Court handed down a very brief opinion in the *Preferred* case. While declining to go as far as the appeals court in extending constitutional protection to cable, the High Court did, for the first time, acknowledge that the medium had some First Amendment standing. The decision was an important one in its recognition of cable as an independent, autonomous medium. But it was a controversial one as well, for while the court agreed that cable had some First Amendment rights, it declined to stipulate what those rights were. In fact, the court appeared to be reaching out for guidance about the nature of the cable communications medium.

Justice Rehnquist, writing for the court, conceded the constitutional questions:

> We do think that the activities in which respondent allegedly seeks to engage plainly implicate First Amendment interests. . . . Cable television partakes of some of the aspects of speech and the communication of ideas as do the traditional enterprises of newspapers, book publishers, public speakers and pamphleteers.[90]

But he went on to state that such rights are not absolute and must be balanced against appropriate countervailing community interests.

> Even protected speech is not equally permissible in all places and at all times. Moreover, where speech and conduct are joined in a single course of action, the First Amendment values must be balanced against competing social interests.[91]

The justice said that before such balancing could take place, however, much more information was needed on the nature of cable, its social role, and its relationship to the cities.

> We are unwilling to decide the legal questions posed by the parties without a more thoroughly developed record of proceedings in which the parties have an opportunity to prove those disputed factual assertions upon which they rely.[92]

Preferred was sent back to the district court for a trial on the facts, one of the most crucial being whether or not cable was a natural monopoly.

As is often the case in law and politics, both sides hailed the decision in *Preferred* as a victory. The industry cited the court's acknowledgement of cable as a First Amendment speaker; the city pointed out the court's desire to examine legitimate needs and interests of the city.

It appeared that the court may have been attempting to strike a First Amendment compromise, balancing the rights of the city with those of the cable operator. Before it was willing to define the essence of that balance, however, the justices wanted to know more about cable TV and to find a logical and rational definition of the medium upon which to base its balancing.

Taken together, the cases of the early and mid-1980s, *Preferred, Quincy, Ferre,* and *Wilkinson,* pointed to a new direction in cable rights that promised cable operators expanded and expanding new First Amendment powers and freedom from government control.

The new judicial chorus was not without some dissonant notes. One or two jurisdictions were still holding on to the concepts set forth in *C.C.C.* and *Burke.* In 1985, for example, a federal district court in Michigan rejected a cable company's complaint that the city violated its constitutional rights by revoking its franchise.[93] The court, in direct opposition to *Preferred*, found economic scarcity and the use of public streets legitimate and powerful rationales in support of government control. But like the decision in *Burke*, the ruling lacked the judicial weight of an appellate level opinion, and, in any event, stood strikingly alone in comparison with the growing number of contrary decisions.

Overall, the direction of case law at those levels seemed to point toward a new model of cable television rights that provided the cable industry with increasing portions of First Amendment protection and continued to nibble away at the edges of cable regulation.

The implications for the industry, for government, and for consumers are obvious and important. Control of access, programming, rates, and general service may begin to shift in ever greater degrees to the company and away from public regulators. The constitutional wisdom of such a movement, and the question of the appropriate First Amendment balance between senders and receivers of cable communications is the subject of the remainder of the book.

Notes

1. 225 F.2d 511 (D.C. Cir. 1955).
2. *Id.* at 517.
3. 321 F.2d 359 (D.C. Cir. 1963).
4. 319 U.S. 190 (1943).
5. 321 F.2d at 364.
6. First Report and Order, 38 F.C.C. 683 (1965).
7. 352 F.2d 729 (D.C. Cir. 1965).
8. 387 F.2d 220 (D.C. Cir. 1967). (A First Amendment challenge to the authority of a municipality to regulate CATV was mounted a year earlier in *Dispatch, Inc. v. City of Erie*, 364 F.2d 539 (3rd Cir. 1966), but the court there declined even to consider the question, stating, "The censorship or free speech issue is underdeveloped and cannot be determined on the present record.")(364 F.2d at 542).
9. 387 F.2d at 225.
10. *Wheeling Antenna Co. v. United States*, 391 F.2d 179, 183 (4th Cir. 1968).
11. 392 U.S. 390 (1968).
12. *Id.* at 399.
13. 399 F.2d 65 (8th Cir. 1968).
14. 394 F.2d 620 (10th Cir. 1968), *cert. denied*, 393 U.S. 858 (1968).
15. 404 F.2d 1187 (3rd Cir. 1968).
16. 394 F.2d at 624.
17. 399 F.2d at 69.
18. 392 U.S. 157 (1968).
19. *Id.* at 178.

20. 411 F.2d 639, 641 (9th Cir. 1969)
21. 302 F. Supp. 652 (N.D. Ohio 1968).
22. *Id.* at 657.
23. 406 U.S. 649 (1972).
24. 415 U.S. 394 (1974).
25. 441 F.2d 1322 (8th Cir. 1971).
26. *Id.* at 1325–26.
27. *C.B.S. v. Teleprompter,* 476 F.2d 338 (2d Cir. 1972).
28. 415 U.S. at 408.
29. *Id.* at 410.
30. *Id.* at 416.
31. 416 F.2d 238 (9th Cir. 1969).
32. *Red Lion Broadcasting v. F.C.C.,* 395 U.S. 367 (1969).
33. 416 F.2d at 241.
34. 406 U.S. at 669.
35. 567 F.2d 9 (D.C. Cir. 1977), *cert. denied* 434 U.S. 829 (1977).
36. *See,* 47 C.F.R. secs. 76.643, 76.225 (1975).
37. 567 F.2d at 49.
38. *Id.* at 44–45.
39. *Id.* at 45 n.80.
40. 418 U.S. 241 (1974).
41. 567 F.2d at 46.
42. 391 U.S. 367 (1968).
43. 567 F.2d at 48.
44. 440 U.S. 689 (1979).
45. Report and Order in Docket No. 20528, 59 F.C.C. 2d 294 (1976).
46. 571 F.2d 1025 (8th Cir. 1978).
47. *Id.* at 1055.
48. *Id.* at 1056.
49. *Id.* at 1054.
50. *Id.* at 1042.
51. *Id.* at 1053.
52. *Id.* 1056.
53. 440 U.S. at 707.
54. 412 U.S. 94 (1973).
55. In footnote 19, (at 709), the Court stated, "The court below suggested that the Commission rules might violate the First Amendment rights of cable operators. Because our decision rests on statutory grounds, we express no view on that question, save to acknowledge that it is not frivolous and to make clear that the asserted constitutional issue did not determine or sharply influence our construction of the statute."
56. *C.C.C. v. Boulder,* 485 F. Supp. 1035 (D. Colo. 1980), *rev'd,* 630 F.2d 704 (10th Cir. 1980) *(Boulder I); C.C.C. v. Boulder,* 496 F. Supp. 823 (D Colo. 1980), *rev'd* 660 F.2d 1370 (10th Cir. 1980), *rev'd* 455 U.S. 40 (1982) *(Boulder II).*
57. *Berkshire Cablevision v. Burke,* 571 F. Supp. 976 (D. R.I. 1983).
58. 630 F.2d at 709.

59. *Id.* at 714.

60. *Id.* at 712.

61. *Id.*

62. *Id.*

63. *Id.* at 714.

64. 660 F.2d at 1377.

65. *Id.* at 1379.

66. *Id.*

67. *Id.*

68. 571 F. Supp. at 985.

69. *Id.* at 985–86.

70. *Id.* at 986–87.

71. 531 F. Supp. 987 (D. Utah 1982).

72. 18 U.S.C. sec. 1464; 47 U.S.C. secs. 503(b), 303(m)(1)(d), 312(a)(6).

73. 438 U.S. 726 (1978).

74. 531 F. Supp. 996.

75. 413 U.S. 15 (1973).

76. 352 U.S. 380 (1957).

77. 555 F. Supp. 1164 (D. Utah 1982).

78. 571 F. Supp. 125 (S.D. Fla. 1983), *aff'd* 755 F.2d 1415 (11th Cir. 1985).

79. 571 F. Supp. at 132.

80. 755 F.2d 1415 (11th Cir. 1985).

81. *Quincy Cable Television v. F.C.C.,* 768 F.2d 1434 (D.C. Cir. 1985).

82. *Id.* at 1449.

83. *Id.* at 1450.

84. *Id.* at 1449.

85. *Preferred Communications, Inc. v. City of Los Angeles,* 754 F.2d 1396 (9th Cir. 1985).

86. *Id.* at n.11.

87. *Id.* at 1404.

88. *Id.* at 1406.

89. *Id.* at 1407–11.

90. *City of Los Angeles v. Preferred Communications* No. 85-390, slip op. at 5–6, (U.S., June 2, 1986).

91. *Id.* at 6.

92. *Id.* at 5.

93. *Carlson v. Village of Union City Michigan,* 601 F. Supp. 801 (W.D. Mich. 1985).

5

Toward a Theory of Cable Rights

The starting point for the development of any model of First Amendment protection for cable must be a broad theoretical consideration of the goals and assumptions of such a model. This implies an overarching theory, or at least a theoretical perspective. This chapter considers alternative theoretical perspectives and suggests a point of view that reconciles some important conflicts embedded in the cable rights dilemma.

Typically, the First Amendment is thought to serve two fundamental purposes: the protection of the individual in his or her expressive activities, and the advancement of the important state interest in the free flow of information. Zechariah Chafee, for example, points out the individual need "of many men to express their opinions on matters vital to them," and the social interest "in the attainment of truth, so that the country may not only adopt the wisest course of action but carry it out in the wisest way."[1]

In its application in the philosophy of the press, the distinction has been described as that between the classical libertarian and social responsibility models. Schramm, Rivers, and Christians explain that the former is grounded in the belief in the supremacy of the individual over the collective, while the latter considers the sanctity of the whole to be paramount.[2]

This dichotomous approach to First Amendment rights has become powerful enough, especially in recent years, to be adopted, at least from an analytical perspective, by some members of the Supreme Court. Justice William Rehnquist, for example, has applied to the two concepts the labels "individualistic" and "utilitarian."[3] The individualistic theory, according to Rehnquist, suggests free speech as an end in itself, sufficiently vital to require constitutional protection. Alternatively, he sees in the utilitarian approach the goal of achieving "certain social purposes," with "the citizen's right to speak [existing] not so much because it benefits him, but because it benefits society."[4]

The justice, while using the dualism to describe approaches to decision making, declines to locate one in a superior position. The same is true for his colleague, Justice Brennan, who creates a dichotomous system, labeling one model a "speech" model and the other a "structural" model.[5] The speech model, according to Brennan, provides protection for the individual against government interference in expressive activities. The structural model considers the social value in according the institutionalized press special protection, but subsequently must balance any competing social interests.[6] It is, therefore, grounded more deeply in societal concerns than is the speech model.

Justice Lewis Powell, unlike his brethren, makes no pretense about neutrality but actively pursues the adoption of a social utility model that would extend special protection to the news media, according to one commentator.[7] Lillian BeVier suggests that Powell has recognized the validity of what she calls the "process-protective" rationale of the First Amendment—a collectivistic conceptualization—and has argued for its application in such cases as *Saxbe v. Washington*.[8] In dissent, Powell advocated a right of special access for the news media to prisons on the grounds of the press's role as a representative of the people in facilitating the exchange of information necessary for the maintenance of the polity.[9]

In some ways that parallel Powell's approach, former Justice Potter Stewart suggested a special institutional protection for the working press not available to the individual operator or pamphleteer.[10] The collective's need for surveillance of its government is the special function of the press, and government is severely limited in its authority to interfere with that function.[11] Individuals, not being representatives of the social good in the same manner, have no similar protection.

When viewed through the filter of these applications, the distinction between the two models is the varying protection that each might provide in different contexts. For example, when weighed against a range of countervailing social interests, one model might extend significantly more protection to speech than the competing model. Alternatively, the two models might be joined in a cooperative effort to counter some attempted governmental interference with expression. In such cases the conjunctive power of the twin rationales becomes exceedingly tenacious when the power of the right of the individual and the interests of society are joined against some infringement by government.

A third situation in which the dualism becomes important is much less easily resolved than the previous two, and is directly involved in the problem of an appropriate First Amendment model for cable. This is the situation in which the two perspectives are challenged not by exogenous social interests, but rather by one another. As the discussion in the previous section has made clear, the competition of social interests in the regulation and protection of cable television most often centers around the problem of whose First Amendment rights are at stake. The question, then, is often cast in this perceived conflict between the First Amendment rights of the collective and the First Amendment rights of the individual. The aforementioned analyses by members of the Supreme Court are illustrative of this conceptualization.

Political philosopher Robert Meister takes a somewhat more sophisticated approach to the problem by considering the complicating factors of institutional representation of claimed First Amendment rights.[12] Meister posits an analytical framework in which either the press or the government might represent the interests of the individual (the part) against the claims on the social collective (the whole). A whole vs. part scenario, therefore, would join the press, as surrogate of the public interest, against the individual, with the individual perhaps represented by the government. Other scenarios find different parties in opposition claiming different representational positions, each scenario requiring different constitutional tests. Despite the complicated factoring of Meister, the central theme of his analysis, like those of the others mentioned above, is essentially dichotomous and therefore nominal; the two chief goals of the First Amendment remain protection of the individual and advancement of the social order.

This dualism is illusory, however, since a closer reading of the Rehnquist and Brennan models, for example, reveals a fogginess of definition and imprecision of language that is characteristic of this approach. Superficial examination suggests the two take similar paths with different labels, but, in fact, Brennan's speech model probably comes closer to the Rehnquist utilitarian model than it does his individualistic model; this is because the speech and utilitarian models both find their form in the protection of individual rights based upon social consequences. Brennan's speech model seeks protection for the individual, in part, because of the social good that will flow from it. His structural model goes beyond even that, however, suggesting special consideration for a social segment (the press) as a representative of the whole. Rehnquist's individualistic model, grounded in the sole justification of personal autonomy, finds no real counterpart in the models of Brennan or Powell. This suggests that the list of, and rationales for, First Amendment protection require, at the very least, categorical expansion. Such expansion is available in the broader First Amendment theories of scholars such as Thomas Emerson and Laurence Tribe.[13] Emerson points to at least four major objectives of his system of freedom of expression: (a) individual self-fulfillment, (b) protection for the process of advancing knowledge and discovering truth, (c) provision for participation by all citizens in society's decision-making process, and (d) maintenance of the balance between consensus and healthy disagreement.[14]

Tribe similarly notes the value inherent in personal autonomy, the protection of the marketplace of ideas, and the advancement of the democratic process.[15] Another First Amendment scholar, Vincent Blasi, adds to this list of First Amendment functions what he calls the "checking value" of the First

Amendment—that is, the so-called watchdog function of the press to monitor and challenge the operations of government.[16]

Such scholars contribute to the analysis by revealing the more subtle nuances of meaning resting in the seemingly simple models of individual versus collective, yet they retain the nominal nature of the categories suggesting some distinct line between the various rationales for protection, and some method of placing these constitutional goals into separate and well-defined categories. It does not seem injudicious to suggest that the dividing lines between these goals are not very distinct and that the difference between protection based on the sanctity of the individual's need for expression and his need for discovering the truth through debate is not very clear-cut. What this suggests is the need for a paradigm of First Amendment rationales based not upon nominal categorization but upon a continuous scale of social value. Examined more closely, the core attribute of the cited goals appears to be the amount of social utility embedded in those goals. A scale might be constructed, therefore, with First Amendment justifications ranging from those totally lacking in social utility—and dependent, therefore, only on individual autonomy—to those totally dependent upon and subservient to social utility. Arranging the major rationales cited above on this scale would give a schematic such as that in figure 5–1.

The continuum finds, at the upper extreme, a rationale for First Amend-

Figure 5–1. The Social Utility Continuum: A Scale of First Amendment Rationales

ment protection emanating from the claimed right of the individual to "speak their piece." Moving further down the social utility scale, one finds protection for speech stemming from the perceived benefits of expression for both the individual and the state in the quest for truth—the so-called marketplace of ideas rationale. Up until this point, First Amendment protection takes the form of sanctions against government interference in nearly every form of speech that might broaden the scope of human thought.

The utilitarian goals point on the continuum protects speech, not on the grounds that to do so would lead to benefits for the state and the individual, but rather because the free flow of information is essential to the proper functioning of the democracy; decisions must be made on the basis of the best and most diverse facts and opinions. Here, media outlets are encouraged to operate under a social responsibility doctrine, and government can work to stimulate the process. Finally, the utilitarian supremacy position flows from a belief that the utilitarian nature of expression is paramount, and the state may take whatever action it feels is justified in protecting and promoting the flow of information, even if it results in the suppression of individual expression.

Various models of free speech can and do find themselves placed at various points along this continuum, drawing strength from greater or lesser portions of the adjacent archetypes. To understand better the roots and ramifications of these various models as they might be applied to cable television, it is useful to examine more closely the philosophical underpinnings, strengths, and weaknesses of approaches drawn from different points along the continuum.

Nonutilitarian Supremacy

Both the nonutilitarian supremacy and the utilitarian consequences archetypes evolve from the major elements of the classical libertarian theory of free speech rights. The roots of this intellectual tradition can be traced back to the Enlightenment and seventeenth and eighteenth century rationalism. Breaking away from the authority of the church, Enlightenment thinkers strove for a secular epistemology. They based their program of knowledge on the "conviction that human understanding is capable, on its own power and without recourse to supernatural assistance, of comprehending the system of the world, and that this new way of understanding the world would lead to a new way of mastering it."[17] Under the elementaristic paradigm, the individual was endowed with God-given natural rights and was the focus of concern, the culture and social structure being defined additively as merely individuals in collusion. The state, therefore, was no more than an institutionalized manifestation of the social interaction of individuals and so served at the combined will of the people. The political system, like the economic system, was seen as self-righting, and benefits would flow to all so long as government maintained its distance from the free and open market place of both goods and ideas.[18]

The twin notions of natural rights and the marketplace of ideas served as guiding principles for the framers of the Constitution and the Bill of Rights. The First Amendment, under the libertarian model, is, therefore, classically interpreted as a prohibition on government interference in the rights of the individual to place his or her views before the community. At the same time, the distinction between these two elements has been recognized and commented upon in judicial decision making.

With respect to the purely nonutilitarian approach of natural rights, the Supreme Court has pointed out the legitimate value and strength in protecting expression for no greater reason than the fulfillment of the individual.[19] Blasi has even suggested seventeenth century theorists found an argument for free speech in man's inability to control either his beliefs or his speech. Lacking such control, men should not be held accountable for their expression.[20]

Other modern scholars have used more conventional arguments to suggest that a strictly nonutilitarian reading of the First Amendment would be the most powerful in protecting freedom of expression. Thomas Scanlon dissects the field into rights based on either institutional forms or moral rights.[21] Scanlon, deriving his view of moral rights from John Stuart Mill, suggests this nonconsequentialist foundation for free speech is independent of any particular set of laws or institutions and, therefore, not subject to their jurisdiction.

A clearer and somewhat more forceful elucidation of this position comes from C. Edwin Baker, who applies to his nominal categorization of the field the labels "classical model," "market failure model," and "liberty model."[22] His classical model is equivalent to the utilitarian consequences archetype. The market failure model gives government the right to intervene in media industry affairs to facilitate expression on the grounds of a monopolized media market, a failure of the assumptions of the libertarian model. The market failure model appears to fall somewhere between the utilitarian goals and utilitarian supremacy points on the social utility continuum. The liberty model is a First Amendment rationale based totally on the right of the individual.

> Speech is protected not as a means to a collective good but because of the value of speech conduct to the individual. The liberty theory justifies protection because of the way the protected conduct fosters individual self-realization and self-determination without improperly interfering with the legitimate claims of others.[23]

Because the liberty model encompasses expressive activity beyond mere speech, it cures the major inadequacies of the marketplace-of-ideas approach without recourse to the more drastic market failure approach, according to Baker.

Finally, Ronald Dworkin argues in favor of a principle-based protection for free speech in contrast with a policy-based rationale. The policy-based protection (a utilitarian consequences/goals archetype) suffers a fatal flaw in that it allows countervailing state interest to be balanced against First Amendment interests, and balancing has never served free speech well, according to Dworkin.[24] He argues that a First Amendment right based solely on the principle of inherent individual rights to expression cannot be so readily balanced (echoing Scanlon) and, therefore, is superior in the protection of expression.

Utilitarian Consequences

The other principal element of the libertarian theory, which is labelled here utilitarian consequences, appears to lack recent champions among the theorists, perhaps because it needs none, as the fundamental justification for most of the important Supreme Court decisions in the free speech area. It is, as Justice Brennan put it, "as comfortable as a pair of old shoes."[25] Nonetheless, in his attempt to define public interest and reconcile it with individual interest, Everette Dennis has provided an interesting new filter through which to view this model, and one particularly fitting to the present examination.[26] Borrowing from Alan Altshuler, he proposed that one way of looking at the social benefits derived from the protection of individual interests is actually captured in the notion of the trickle-down theory.[27]

While Dennis discusses this concept in a slightly different context, the image of protected individual expression filtering down and manifesting itself in second and third order social effects is readily transferable to the utilitarian consequences archetype and serves to illuminate the meaning and application of the approach.

A more eloquent statement of the position came in the 1971 Supreme Court decision, *Cohen v. California,* in which the court noted that the First and Fourteenth Amendments removed government restraints from the arena of public discussion, putting the decision as to what views shall be voiced largely into the hands of each of us in the hope that use of such freedom will ultimately produce a more capable citizenry and a more perfect polity.[28]

Under this archetype, then, individual speech is protected, in part, because to do so will eventually benefit the community.

Utilitarian Goals

Unlike the utilitarian consequences approach, which suggests that protection of the individual's right to speak will lead to prosocial consequences, the utilitarian goals approach starts with a concern for the collective, suggesting benefits that will eventually accrue to the individual. In short, it reverses the utilitarian consequences equation. However, this need not imply a lack of concern for the rights of the individual; the importance of providing an opportunity for individual expression and protecting the same from state intervention remains a significant value. It is, however, secondary to the greater good that is seen to flow from systemic protection provided the community.

The philosophical roots of this approach, and the utilitarian supremacy position, go back to Hegel, who conceived of the social history of man as a living, spiritual whole.[29] The myriad interactions of man within his culture were reified and aggregated and the product given a life of its own.

In his development of sociology, Comte took up this collectivistic strand in Hegel's formulation[30] and helped make the analogy of society as an organism or entity whose whole was greater than the sum of its parts, the dominant paradigm for sociology from the Spencerian theories of the late 1800s to the structure-functionalism of Parsons in the mid-1900s.[31] The concept also was adopted by political theorists such as the English idealists T.H. Green and Francis Bradley and, of course, the Marxists. For the English idealists, individual rights were neither inherent nor natural; they were the product of the general will of the collective. The state secured for individuals certain powers in dealing with other citizens, and individuals were required to act as socially responsible agents in accordance with socially established rights and duties.

This broader social theory was applied to expression in the form of the social responsibility theory of the press and, by implication, into a collectivistic theory of First Amendment protection.[32] So, as the major trends in political and sociological thinking were shifting from the individualistic to collectivistic paradigms through the late nineteenth and early twentieth centuries, Rivers, Schramm, and Christians argue that popular thinking about the press was shifting apace, claiming:

> John Locke's philosophy of inherent rights and rational man has been challenged by modern philosophy, which is inclined to doubt the concept of natural law on which the notion rests, and by modern psychology, which has identified many areas of irrationality in man and cast considerable doubt on his ability to distinguish truth from skillful propaganda. Classical laissez-faire economics has been challenged by the belief that interfering with the operation of the market enables us to avoid disastrous troughs of the busi-

ness cycle. . . . The self-righting process has received forceful attack as too unrealistic and romanticized. In short, our view of man and our view of society are altogether less optimistic than they were in the Enlightenment.[33]

The trends described by Schramm, et al., climaxed in 1947 with the publication of the Hutchin's Commission Report on Freedom of the Press,[34] the Magna Carta of social responsibility theory. It called for a program of fairness, accuracy, and a dedication by the press to the welfare of the community. Its chief author, William Hocking, urged a self-policing action by the journalistic community but cautioned that, should the press fail to clean its own house, government might be tempted to intercede, and justifiably so.[35]

This notion of self-policing is important, for it helps distinguish the two collectivistic types on the social utility continuum. It is assumed, or at least strongly encouraged, that the press and its individual members, exercising their rights of expression will do so in socially responsible ways, that they are, in fact, capable of doing so, and that government will exercise maximum restraint in tampering with the system so long as such goals are honored. Mechanisms for fostering and reinforcing this approach are very important for those who advocate this form of balance between the rights of the collective and the rights of the individual, and normally include educational programs and nongovernmental media watchdog agencies of some sort.[36] As will be discussed shortly, government, under the utilitarian supremacy approach, is much less hesitant to take an active role in the control of expression.

Perhaps the sharpest example of First Amendment theory flowing from this perspective came from Alexander Meiklejohn in his early theory of First Amendment protection. For Meiklejohn, the First Amendment was a protection for political speech only, the aim being the smooth and proper functioning of the democratic process.[37] Government is forbidden to interfere in the expression of political ideas, but this does not mean that everyone who wishes to speak may do so under the umbrella of the First Amendment. According to Meiklejohn, "What is essential is not that everyone shall speak, but that everything worth saying shall be said."[38] The idea is protected, not the individual.

This primary concern with the flow of ideas that will advance the social good does not, however, forsake completely the value of individual self-fulfillment through expression. According to Meiklejohn, this good is provided for, but not under the sanction of the First Amendment; it is protected by the Fifth Amendment's due process clause insuring life, liberty, and property. This right of personal speech is, of course, of lesser value than speech that adds to the efficient functioning of society and, therefore, may be balanced against other social goods. But when balanced against the collective expression protected by the First Amendment it must lose, for such expression is, under Meiklejohn's theory, protected absolutely.[39]

While Meiklejohn has been criticized for reading too narrowly the protection extended by the First Amendment,[40] his general position illustrates an approach that would fall somewhere near the utilitarian goals archetype on the social utility continuum, for it recognizes value in individual expression but is willing to override that value, with the greater good present, in expression that serves the polity.

An illustrative application of this approach might be the societal function model attributed to Justice Powell. Special rights are extended to the press on the basis of the social value that will result from the increased flow of information. While similar privileges are not provided for individuals, neither is it suggested that the press' special status would override individual First Amendment protection should the two come into conflict. In this way Powell strikes a more even balance in the contest between social and individual rights than does even Meiklejohn, but the approach, nonetheless, suggests a more collectivistically oriented program than the utilitarian consequences type.

Utilitarian Supremacy

The more extreme variant of the collectivistic philosophy, the utilitarian supremacy ideal type, is much less willing to recognize the value of expression based on inherent individual rights, or at least is less willing to accord them weight when balancing them against the rights of the whole. This approach grants government greater powers in manipulating the communications system in order to achieve specified goals of information access. It is closer to Baker's market failure theory than the less intrusive utilitarian goals archetype, and serves as the foundation for arguments that economic control of the means of communication in society justify state intervention to secure information and speech benefits for everyone.

Jerome Barron operates from this perspective in his argument in favor of state enforced access to newspapers.[41] Barron rejects the libertarian philosophies as unrealistically romantic and practically irrelevant in our modern economic system. He also implies that the weaker social responsibility variant of the utilitarian perspective is insufficient to insure the requisite diversity of opinion and ideology (perhaps because it is relatively unenforceable in this context). The First Amendment rights of newspapers must, therefore, give way to the superior First Amendment rights of the collective, making state-mandated access to these important vehicles of expression permissible, even vital.

In his advocacy of enforced access to the press, Barron points to similar requirements for the broadcast media, which serves as an example of an application of First Amendment rights that moves closer to the utilitarian supremacy end of the continuum. Government here exhibits significant control in all aspects of the communications industry. A closer examination of the application of this First Amendment principle is reserved for later discussion. It is enough to point out now that the Supreme Court has concluded that, in general:

> [T]he people as a whole retain their interest in free speech by radio and their collective right to have the medium function consistently with the ends and purposes of the First Amendment. It is the right of the viewers and the listeners, not the right of the broadcasters, which is paramount.[42]

An even stronger utilitarian position might provide for total government control over the means of communication as the best method for facilitating the goals and purposes of the First Amendment. Individual rights to freedom of expression might be discounted as relatively irrelevant under such a system. The logical extreme of such a system might be embraced in a socialist state where the government works with the press toward understood and accepted social goals.

Toward an Equitable Protection Model

Each of the points along the continuum—social consequence, nonutilitarian goals, and so forth—suggests a model of First Amendment rights: an archetype based upon its relative commitment to the social utility served by those rights. The central problem in any model that swings too far toward one end or another of the continuum is its failure to provide for the legitimate interests in the competing positions. Models that suggest a system of protection based chiefly on particularistic assumptions, therefore, neglect the important values contained in a concern for the whole—values which might not be accommodated in an elementaristic perspective. Alternatively, collectivistic theories often appear to permit the restraint of individual expressive activities in the name of the people, in spite of compelling arguments that individuals ought to be protected in their desire to express themselves even if such expression does not necessarily serve to enhance discourse valued by others. Tribe considers this problem in the development of his approach to First Amendment values, stating that narrowly defined models such as those considered here are, in the end, insufficient to provide full protection to expression:

> No satisfactory jurisprudence of free speech can be built upon such partial or compromised notions of the bases for expressional protection or the

boundaries of the conduct to be protected. However tempting it may be to resist governmental claims for restricting speech by retreating to an artificially narrowed zone and then defending it without limit, any such course is likely in the end to sacrifice too much to strategic maneuver; the claims for suppression will persist, and the defense will be no stronger for having to withdraw to arbitrarily constricted territory. Any adequate conception of freedom of speech must instead draw upon several strands of theory in order to protect a rich variety of expressional modes.[43]

It is, or course, possible to draw on all the important strands of theory only when developing a model of First Amendment protection concerned exclusively with the protection of expression from governmental interference. Tribe does not seem to take up the task of dealing with the so-called affirmative theories—which are essential in the discussion of cable rights— and, therefore, fails to see that varying perspectives can come into conflict. He does advance the discussion, however, by implying the need to seek the greatest possible protection for all the competing values and goals of the First Amendment, even if that means a delicate balancing act to assure such comprehensive protection.

The goal, then, of any model should be to provide as much protection as possible for both the individual and the collective, to seek to accommodate all degrees of social utility. That requires occasional balancing when goals conflict, but it is suggested here that cable may be uniquely suited to provide the greatest protection for all interests with very little reciprocal suppression of one goal for another. The problem is the fashioning of an equitable protection model of First Amendment rights applicable to the peculiar medium of cable television. In theory, it would satisfy the demands associated with nearly all points on the social utility continuum, or at least be superior to any alternative models in this respect. In considering various models that could achieve this goal, two issues become important: the satisfaction of the theoretical needs and the ability to meet practical considerations.

The theoretical aspects are chiefly the ones described above: providing protection for First Amendment interests associated with multiple points on the continuum. The practical aspects have not been as fully discussed but are equally important. In practice, the social utility continuum, as noted, has been taken as a dichotomous equation pitting the interests of the individual against those of the collective. The traditional, accepted model of First Amendment rights is that associated with the social consequences approach, essentially a form of individualist orientation. The enforcement elements of this model are essentially prophylactic in nature; they are the so-called negative powers of the First Amendment which prevent government from interfering in expressive activity.

Models drawn from the far social goals end of the continuum are often concerned with the government's role in advancing expression rather than with government's role in its suppression. Such models invoke the so-called affirmative measures advocated by Barron. This approach is of modern and largely untested mettle, however, and in contests with individualistic models generally has been the loser. Such is the lesson of *Tornillo*. In most cases, the Supreme Court has held in favor of a collectivistic model only when some additional element, some special circumstance, is present. Broadcasting is the pre-eminent example. A variety of special circumstances in broadcasting (e.g., impact, scarcity, fiduciary responsibility) have been cited in declaring the rights of society to be superior to the rights of the indvidual. Without such special circumstances, however, it seems difficult for collectivistically oriented rights to prevail over individually oriented rights in modern First Amendment law.

The practical problem for the equitable protection model for cable, then, is the assertion of some special circumstance that would be sufficient to support the claims of First Amendment rights flowing from a strong social utility interest. While an even balancing of individual and collective rights is sought in theory, an additional practical element, such as scarcity, seems necessary to supplement the asserted social interests. Given this fact, the problem becomes one of analyzing the various explicitly and implicitly proposed models of cable rights and measuring them with respect to both theoretical and practical considerations. Do they adequately satisfy the demands from all points of the continuum and do they provide a legitimate framework of special circumstances that would make the necessary balancing possible?

Summary

Models grounded at different places along the social utility continuum derive their raison d'être from different mixes of societal and individual values and produce proportionately varying protection for those values. An equitable protection model strives for the greatest amount of protection and the least amount of interference with the rights of the individual and the rights of the collective. Various models of First Amendment rights, springing from different positions on the continuum, have been applied differentially to specific communication technologies. The task with respect to cable television is to examine each of these models and determine the extent to which they would fulfill the requirements of the equitable protection approach if they were applied to the technology of cable TV.

Subsequent chapters, therefore, will examine the forms of protection classically associated with different communications technologies as they might be applied to cable. The consequences of such applications will be considered in three dimensions: content, structure, and behavior. Through such analysis a new model, based upon both the aims of the equitable protection approach and the unique qualities of cable television, may be constructed.

Notes

1. Z. Chafee, *Free Speech in the United States,* at 33 (Cambridge, MA: Harvard University Press, 1941).

2. W. Rivers, W. Schramm and C. Christians, *Responsibility in Mass Communications* (New York: Harper and Row, 3d ed., 1980).

3. W. Rehnquist, "The First Amendment Freedom, Philosophy and the Law," 12 *Gonz. L. Rev.* 1 (1976).

4. *Id* at 3.

5. Justice Brennan, Address at the dedication of the Samuel Newhouse Law Center, Rutgers University, Oct. 17, 1979, *see,* 32 *Rutgers L. Rev.* 173 (1979).

6. *Id.* at 176–77.

7. *See,* L. BeVier, "Justice Powell and the First Amendment's 'Societal Function': A Preliminary Analysis," 68 *Va. L. Rev.* 177 (1982).

8. 417 U.S. 843 (1974) (Powell, J., dissenting).

9. *Id.* at 862–64.

10. *See,* J. Stewart, "Or of the Press," 26 *Hastings Law Journal* 631 (1975).

11. *Zurcher v. Stanford Daily,* 436 U.S. 547 (1978) (Stewart, J. dissenting).

12. R. Meister, "Journalistic Silence and Governmental Speech: Can Institutions Have Rights?," 16 *Harv. C.R.-C.L. L. Rev.* 319 (1981).

13. T. Emerson, *The System of Freedom of Expression,* (New York: Random House, 1970); L. Tribe, *American Constitutional Law,* (Mineola, NY: Foundation Press, 1975).

14. Emerson, *supra* at 6–7.

15. Tribe, *supra* at 576–79.

16. Unlike others, Blasi does not rely on this checking value as one component of a dualistic system, but rather sees it as supplementary to a system based on multiple constitutional aims; *see* V. Blasi, The Checking Value in First Amendment Theory, 1977 *A.B. Found. Research J.* 521.

17. E. Cassirer, *The Enlightenment,* in *Encyclopedia of the Social Sciences,* vol. 5 at 547 (New York: MacMillian Publishing, 1935).

18. A. Smith, *The Wealth of Nations* (New York: The Modern Library, 1937).

19. *See, Whitney v. Calif.,* 274 U.S. 357, 375 (1927).

20. Blasi, *supra,* at 544–45.

21. T. Scanlon, "A Theory of Freedom of Expression," 1 *Philosophy and Public Affairs* 204 (1971).

22. C. E. Baker, "Scope of the First Amendment Freedom of Speech," 25 *U.C.L.A. L. Rev.* 964 (1978).

23. *Id.* at 966.

24. R. Dworkin, "Is the Press Losing the First Amendment?," *New York Review of Books,* Dec. 4, 1980, at 49.

25. Brennan, *supra.*

26. E. Dennis, "The Press and the Public Interest: A Definitional Dilemma," 23 *DePaul L. Rev.* 937 (1974).

27. *See,* A. Altshuler, "The Potential of Trickle Down," 15 *The Public Interest* 46 (1969).

28. 403 U.S. 15, 24 (1971).

29. *See,* G. Hegel, *The Philosophy of History* (New York: Dover Publications, 1956).

30. A. Comte, *The Positive Philosophy of Auguste Comte* (London: J. Chapman, 1853).

31. *See generally,* D. Martindale, *The Nature and Types of Sociological Theory* 67–107, 441–495 (Boston: Houghton Mifflin Co., 2d ed., 1981).

32. *See generally,* Rivers, Schramm, and Christians, *supra.*

33. *Id.* at 44.

34. Commission on Freedom of the Press, *A Free and Responsible Press* (Chicago: University of Chicago Press, 1947).

35. *See,* W. Hocking, *Freedom of the Press: A Framework of Principle* (Chicago: University of Chicago, 1947).

36. *See, e.g.,* J. E. Gerald, *The Social Responsibility of the Press* (Minneapolis: University of Minnesota Press, 1963). (Gerald urges stronger educational programs in journalistic ethics, and E. Dennis, *supra,* suggests a three-level model of reinforcement that provides for government intervention only as a last resort.)

37. A. Meiklejohn, *Political Freedom: The Constitutional Powers of the People* (New York: Harper and Bros., 1960) (In his later years, Meiklejohn amended his position to extend First Amendment protection to artistic, philosophical, educational, and scientific speech as well. *See,* J. Kalven, "Robert Bork and the Constitution," 264, *The Nation,* 1 (October 1983).)

38. *Id.* at 26.

39. Although in the end, the theory appears to resemble a traditional "clear and present danger" test rather than the truly absolute position suggested by Meiklejohn's rhetoric. *See, e.g.,* his testimony before the 1955 Senate Subcommittee on Constitutional Rights, Meiklejohn at 122.

40. *See, e.g.,* Tribe, *supra,* at 577–78.

41. J. Barron, *Freedom of the Press for Whom?* (Bloomington, IN: Indiana University Press, 1973).

42. *Red Lion Broadcasting v. F.C.C.,* 395 U.S. 367, 390 (1969).

43. Tribe, *supra,* at 579.

6
The Broadcast Model

I t is logical to begin the discussion by examining the broadcast model, for throughout its regulatory history, cable has been most closely associated with that medium. Cable began its constitutional evolution as an ancillary broadcast service, was defined in terms of its relationship with broadcasting, and drew its regulatory life from the broadcasting experience. Most cable rule making followed broadcast precedent, and the federal restrictions on content, structure, and behavior reflect the experience with and the philosophy behind the regulation of over-the-air TV.

Philosophically, the goals of the broadcast model are first and foremost the protection of the free flow of information to the public. This is a central point in *Red Lion Broadcasting v. F.C.C.* The case provides a nearly pure statement of the utilitarian goals archetype in Justice White's majority opinion:

> It is the purpose of the First Amendment to preserve an uninhibited marketplace of ideas in which truth will ultimately prevail, rather than to countenance monopolization of the market, whether it be by government itself or by a private licensee. . . . It is the right of the public to receive suitable access to social, political, aesthetic, moral and other ideas and experiences which is crucial here.[1]

This is not to imply that the communicator is totally without rights under the broadcast model. There is a margin of protection afforded the broadcaster, a degree of editorial discretion that cannot be manipulated by the government or by competing private interests. In *C.B.S. v. D.N.C.*, a majority of the Supreme Court noted that determining how a broadcaster best serves the public interest was the job of the broadcaster, not the listener or the state. "Editing is what editors are for," stated Chief Justice Burger.[2] In the end, however, when the rights of the editor to edit have been balanced against the rights of the public to receive diverse opinions, the communicator's rights have given way.[3] So, to the extent that some in industry may have seen *C.B.S. v. D.N.C.* as a blow for increased broadcaster autonomy, they were disabused of that notion in *C.B.S. v. F.C.C.* in 1981, when the Supreme Court attempted to clarify its holding that *Red Lion* was the rule and *D.N.C.* the exception:

> Although the broadcast industry is entitled under the First Amendment to exercise "the widest journalistic freedom consistent with its public duties," the Court has made it clear that "[i]t is the right of the viewers and listeners, not the right of the broadcasters which is paramount."[4]

On the social utility continuum, the broadcast model, therefore, falls somewhere within the social goals range. What, then, are the implications of this model for control of cable industry structure, behavior, and program content?

Application of the Model

General Jurisdiction

Under the broadcast model, government, in the first instance, asserts general jurisdiction over the communicator and requires him or her to obtain a license to operate.[5] This licensing requirement, the Supreme Court has determined, does not offend the First Amendment. As Justice Thurgood Marshall explained in *F.C.C. v. N.C.C.B.*:

> Requiring those who wish to obtain a broadcast license to demonstrate that such would serve the public interest does not restrict the speech of those who are denied licenses; rather it preserves the interests of "the people as a whole."[6]

Similar federal approval has been required of the cable communicator,[7] and, in contrast with the broadcaster, the FCC has, in the past, also required that cable operators obtain some form of local governmental approval to operate.[8] Further, even after dropping that requirement, the commission continued for several years to offer guidelines on franchising for local communities.[9] In addition, cable often has had to acquire formal state permission to operate. There has been, in short, a general licensing system in cable that has not only mimicked, but surpassed, the broadcast model.

Structure

Structural considerations deal principally with ownership. The functional core of the broadcast model is the inability of everyone who wishes to own a broadcast station to do so. The government, as representative of the people, must determine the guidelines for ownership of the communications system. Even though it necessarily prevents many who would wish to speak through this medium from doing so, the balance must be struck in favor of the rights of the society. As it has been applied to radio and television, the broadcast model permits the federal government to set tight restrictions on the nature and character of individuals who may be issued licenses,[10] it determines the kinds of properties individuals may own in any given geographic area,[11] and it determines the distribution of broadcast properties among various markets.[12] Such regulations have led to the social control of ownership on the basis of property interests in adjacent media as well.[13]

As the guiding model in cable regulation, such restrictions have similarly been applied to that medium. Upon the suggestion of the federal government, local jurisdictions have customarily granted cable franchises (licenses) for a limited period, usually fifteen years.[14] Ownership restrictions parallel those in radio and television, with municipal consideration given to the character and financial history of the applicant,[15] often with preference to partial local ownership.

Ownership of alternative media also has affected the granting of a cable license,[16] although the trend is toward relaxation of such restrictions. While the FCC has declined to limit the number of cable operations an individual may own, such controls have been considered[17] and there appears to be nothing within the broadcast model to suggest First Amendment barriers to such control. The broadcast model also implies authority at the state level to limit the number of cable companies in a given area, but while several states have made such provisions,[18] it is generally assumed that the economic realities of cablecasting obviate setting statutory guidelines.

Access, too, is a form of structural control. While the Supreme Court has strictly limited the FCC's power to promulgate access rules for both broadcasting and cable,[19] it has done so primarily through interpretation of statutory law and legislative intent. Where Congress has narrowly acted to mandate access, the court has been reluctant to interfere. Provisions granting certain political candidates[20] or private individuals attacked by a broadcast station[21] a right to free or purchased airtime, therefore, have been applied equally to broadcasters and local origination channels on cable systems.[22] Without clear Congressional or regulatory guidance, the court has declined to approve requests initiated by citizens for broadcast access, invoking the limited First Amendment protection granted the station owner.[23] This suggests some attempt at balancing rights and makes suspect, at least under the broadcast model, the routine application of access requirements to cable systems by state and local authorities.

Structurally, then, the broadcast model appears to provide the state with significant power to determine ownership patterns in a given communications industry on the philosophical basis of allocating scarce or monopoly outlets to divergent, and hopefully, representative community voices. Access to the system may be permitted in the presence of clear legislative direction and demonstrated state need, but must be weighed against the limited editorial autonomy of the system operator.

Behavior

In contrast to nonutilitarian models of First Amendment rights, the broadcast model authorizes state control of numerous noncontent aspects of communicator behavior. In broadcasting, such regulations have ranged from simple directives regarding operating hours of a station[24] to more complicated requirements governing contractual and other business arrangements with program suppliers and networks,[25] regulations that go beyond the normal application of labor or antitrust laws. The scope of state power here has been extended to permit the denial of a license to applicants whose parent companies may have been found to engage in illegal or unethical business practices.[26] Broadcasters, in the recent past, have been required to maintain operating logs for public inspection[27] and to report on progress in fulfilling expectations of the Equal Employment Opportunity Act.[28] One former obligation, onerous in the eyes of the broadcasters, was the requirement which directed broadcasters to survey their audiences to determine important community issues and then present formal programming proposals to address those topics. This was an obligation imposed on the basis of the medium's role in facilitating the exchange of important social information.

The behavioral controls applied to cable by the federal government have been minimal and include the maintenance of operating records,[29] compliance with Equal Employment Opportunities guidelines,[30] ownership restrictions,[31] and adherence to various technical standards.[32] They are not as extensive as those imposed on broadcasters, but the model does not imply lesser requirements than those for broadcasters. Behavioral restrictions placed on cable operators by state and local authorities often have reached far beyond the federal limitations on broadcasters, and have included financial reporting obligations,[33] construction requirements,[34] and special community service obligations such as area interconnect capacity.[35]

Nowhere is local behavioral control more apparent, and more vehemently protested, than in rate regulation. Despite government authority under the Interstate Commerce Clause, neither Congress nor the FCC has ever moved to establish operating rates for broadcasters. Yet local agencies have regularly required cable operators to justify rates charged to subscribers for hookup and service, with such authority often codified at the state level.[36] (A key concern of the cable industry, in pushing passage of the Cable Act, was inclusion of a provision restricting local authority over subscriber rates.)

The constitutional validity of such behavioral controls under the broadcast model probably would have to be determined by balancing the nonutilitarian interests of the system operator with the collective interests of the society, with an a priori assumption of special weight for the utilitarian goals of the system. Where such restrictions exceeded those normally associated with the legitimate regulation of commercial activity and imposed upon the free speech interests of the system operator, special sensitivity would have to be accorded the rights of the licensee.

Content

It is clear from *C.B.S. v. F.C.C.* that the broadcast model extends a limited degree of autonomy to communicators, but that autonomy is circumscribed by the greater good that must accrue to the public. This general philosophical direction is apparent not only in structural and behavioral controls, but also in permissibly proscribed content.

The parameters of content control under a broadcast model may be traced by allusion to four content categories: overall programming, political speech, commercial speech, and indecent speech.

The limits of communicator autonomy may be best illustrated by those regulations that have been aimed at overall programming, specifically, the cases involving program format and balanced programming. The debate over the appropriate role of government in determining radio station formats vividly presents the juxtaposition of individual and collective interests. Despite the FCC's reluctance to inject itself into this area, the federal courts in *Citizens Committee to Preserve the Voice of the Arts v. F.C.C.*[37] and *WEFM v. F.C.C.*[38] instructed the commission to consider the public interest associated with a station abandoning a unique format. The commission saw, among other problems, a potential threat to the First Amendment rights of the communicator, but the appellate court was adamant about protecting the rights of listeners to receive diverse voices. Upon review, the Supreme Court upheld the position of the FCC and the broadcasters that such content decisions were best left up to the licensee.[39] But the difficulty of the question suggests that communicator independence reaches its outermost limit here. Such a feeling is reinforced by Justice Byron White's cautionary comment in the majority opinion that the FCC should "be alert to the consequences of its policies and should stand ready to alter its rule if necessary to preserve the public interest more fully.[40]

The clear implication from *C.B.S. v. F.C.C.* is the continued dominance of the social utility approach to broadcast regulation, with the communicator given latitude, within governmentally designated boundaries, to achieve certain goals. Given the markedly different characteristics of the medium, it is unlikely that format controls would even be attempted in the area of cable.

Other extensions of the broadcast doctrine in this category may not be so farfetched, however.

The FCC, at one time, required communicators under the broadcast model to provide balanced programming in the course of their license period,[41] recommending that news, public affairs, sports, religious, and agricultural programs, among others, be part of the programming week. In formulating this policy, the commission specifically noted the First Amendment role of the communicator, eschewing day-to-day oversight of station programming, but maintaining a general communicator obligation to program in the public interest, as defined by the commission.

Would it be possible for government to impose similar guidelines on cable in the form of a general responsibility to program channels to satisfy a wide variety of public interests? While this is certainly the practical business aim of cablecasters and can easily be accommodated on larger systems, only a minority of cable systems in the country now have more than twenty or thirty channels, and a balanced cable menu might necessitate unwanted changes in smaller systems. While presenting numerous regulatory and economic questions, a balanced channel allocation directive would certainly not fall outside the boundaries of the broadast model and, in fact, might be seen as analogous to structural access requirements which are now a part of everyday cable life.

Political speech restrictions in the form of Fairness and Equal Opportunity obligations remain a part of the regulatory framework (despite the ongoing political efforts to remove them), and attach to cablecasting as well as broadcasting.[42]

Were the broadcast model to find constitutional support in its application to cable, continued extension of content-oriented political speech rules to cable would certainly be defensible, although they might, nonetheless, be abandoned in favor of structural access controls.

With respect to commercial speech, all of the regulatory and legislative restrictions that apply to the print media extend to broadcasting as well. Given the reduced force of individual rights under the broadcast model, however, additional restraints may be imposed on the communicator. FCC rules, therefore, have required broadcasters to concern themselves with commercial identification,[43] commercial volume,[44] subliminal advertising,[45] and the use of sound effects in advertisements.[46]

The courts have held that the Fairness Doctrine may apply to commercial messages when such messages constitute a controversial issue of public importance, and further, that there may be an affirmative First Amendment obligation on the part of the government to assure that broadcast time is made available for replies to such messages,[47] although discretion as to the general applicability of the Fairness Doctrine to advertising has been left up to the FCC.[48] Moreover, Congress has, in the case of cigarettes, expressly forbidden the communication of commercial messages on television and radio.[49] In upholding the ban, the federal district court claimed that the constitutional power under the Interstate Commerce Clause was sufficient to justify such an order in any medium, but that "the unique characteristics of electronic communication make it especially subject to regulation in the public interest."[50] And in this case, the determinative distinction between the justification for the rule in broadcasting and the lack of need for such a rule in print appeared to be the ubiquity and influence of the former medium. The court explained: "Substantial evidence showed that the most persuasive advertising was being conducted on radio and television, and that these broadcasts were particularly effective in reaching a very large audience of young people."[51]

Unlike most other aspects of broadcast regulation, commercial speech is one area in which the states have been significantly active. Sadowski found forty-three states which passed laws governing areas of advertising affecting broadcasters.[52] The now defunct Oklahoma laws prohibiting the advertisement of liquor are illustrative of the broadcast model's treatment of commercial speech and its application to cable. Under this model, an assumption is made that the double force of a second-tier position for both commercial speech and cable speech would make state regulation of this content particularly safe from challenges based on nonutilitarian First Amendment arguments.

Finally, on the basis of service in the public interest, convenience and necessity, the FCC has sanctioned numerous and isolated varieties of speech. The legal problems raised by the increasing incidence of sexually explicit films on cable already have been discussed. The broadcast model plainly provides for the restriction of sexually oriented material that would receive First Amendment protection under the print model. Even when the speech involved has little or no relation to the prurient interest element in the judicial definition of obscenity, and is merely deemed unfit for a public setting, protection of the public interest may outweigh the value of expression protected only by the possibility of self-fulfillment. *In re WUHY-FM*, for example, a radio station was chastized for broadcasting an interview that contained the expletives shit and fuck.[53] Similarly, the state may constitutionally pressure communicators to monitor even the music they play to prevent the distribution of cultural symbols that might encourage or condone activity the government deems to be antisocial.[54]

The application of broadcastlike content controls for cable in situations involving commercial or other nonutilitarian forms of speech is more troubling than similar applications for political speech, because the intent of the former appears to be suppression while the intent of the latter is increased access to ideas. The limits of suppression under the broadcast model are quite unclear in nonpolitical areas. The potential for state and local authority to prohibit a variety of content forms seems open-ended. New York State once proposed a law which would require the cablecaster to check the flow of material that might be classified as indecent violence.[55] Might smaller, rural communities prohibit the distribution of programming that examines or possibly advocates variant lifestyles or radical political ideologies? When speech forms that maintain only a secondary constitutional position are distributed over a communications system provided collectivistically oriented First Amendment status, the limits of government control are broad and vague.

Critique

The dangers hidden in the combined extension of the commercial speech doctrine and the broadcast model to cable are representative of the broader philosophical problem of applying this approach to cable. While the broadcast model does provide some security for those values suggested by the non-utilitarian and utilitarian goals archetypes, it seems to suggest that provision for those values will be afforded only so long as they do not conflict with the countervailing values embedded in the utilitarian goals perspective. That is, the individual rights of the communicator to express divergent and or unpleasant ideas, even messages that from the collectivistic point of view are valueless, are honored only to the point that they do not conflict with the social goals of the communication system established by the state. Individual rights are honored, that is, only in the rhetoric of regulation; in practice there is no substantial protection for the owner and operator of the system.

Furthermore, the important element of content neutrality, which must be a dominant theme in any model that hopes to secure full protection for all parties, is missing. Formally, the FCC is statutorily prohibited from interfering with the free speech rights of the licensed communicator. According to section 326 of the Communications Act:

> Nothing in this act shall be understood or construed to give the Commission the power of censorship over radio communications or signals transmitted by any radio station, and no regulation or condition shall be promulgated or fixed by the Commission which shall interfere with the right of free speech by means of radio communication.[56]

But despite this plainly worded admonition, the history of FCC regulation speaks loudly to the hollowness of the language. Suppression of speech based solely on content has been exercised regularly, and approved of by the courts, on the basis of the medium-dependent variable First Amendment rights. With regard to the balance struck between the rights expressed through the nonutilitarian end of the social utility continuum and those expressed at the utilitarian supremacy end, the broadcast model appears to place little value on the rights of individual expression. On this basis alone, it could be rejected as an appropriate model for cable television. But other, more practical problems exist as well. These have to do with the necessary lever by which the collectivistic values are asserted over the elementaristic values in the first instance.

Fundamental to the application of affirmative rights of the public is, as discussed in the previous chapter, some showing of special circumstances that warrant overturning the traditional supremacy of the nonutilitarian and utilitarian consequences model of individual protection. In broadcasting, these special circumstances have included the scarcity of the airwaves, public ownership of the spectrum, and the impact or ubiquity of the medium. In cable, application of the broadcast model has been premised on the doctrine of some special relationship between cable and over-the-air television—the so-called ancillarity doctrine.

As has been noted, the use of the scarce resource rationale to justify government control of broadcasting and cablecasting has been the subject of much judicial and scholarly comment, most of it unfavorable. The validity of the theory in its application to broadcasting is not at issue here, and the history of judicial discussion of its applicability to cable has been traced in previous chapters. It is sufficient at this point to note briefly that the argument of the use of scarcity to breach individual rights has been asserted and countered in two dimensions, the claim of a limited number of channels of communication and a naturally limited number of controlling voices.

The first claim is specious. The promise of cable as a medium of abundance is its oldest and most advertised claim. While no outer limits have been set on the meaning of natural scarcity (perhaps even thirty channels in a town is insufficient to meet expressive needs), all elements in nature are finite, and the natural limit on the number of acres planted in lumber does not serve to justify government control of the print medium. The courts and the regulators have noted for a long time that scarcity of channels is insufficient justification for the regulation of cable, and this rationale appears to be growing less reasonable with every advance in the technology.

The limit to the number of voices refers to the argument that cable systems should be the unit of measure rather than cable channels for, unlike channels, the number of systems in a given area seems to be naturally restricted. This argument must be distinguished at the outset from the corollary position which suggests an economic limit to the number of competing companies, an issue that will be discussed at length in chapter 7. The notion that some physical barrier exists to the number of wires that can be strung throughout a city lacks the solid foundation of fact. When too many broadcast signals are forced into a given range in the radio spectrum, the result is interference. There is no analogy to this in cablecasting; wires strung in large groups may become unsightly, but they will not be functionally altered. Several courts, most recently the appeals court in *Preferred*, have noted this,[57] and many cities and states acknowledge it by providing for nonexclusive franchises.[58] Co-extensive, competing cable systems are, furthermore, rare but not unknown.[59] The notion of physical scarcity in either ownership or channels appears now to be an abandoned justification for government regulation of cable.

Closely akin to the scarcity argument in broadcast regulation is the proposal that the airwaves are a public resource and licensees are keepers of the public trust. It suggests a fiduciary role for those granted limited permission for use of the public domain. The question that arises in extending this argument to cablecasting is that of identifying the pertinent public or natural resource. Cable communication utilizes copper wires or fiber optics that are run underground or along poles to subscriber homes. It is unlikely that the actual wires could be considered within the public domain. But the use of public streets, alleyways, and thoroughfares has been advanced as a justification for state control. Where the stringing and maintenance of wires presents a public disturbance there is no question about the right of the appropriate local agency to regulate such disturbance so that it is kept to a minimum. As the appellate court pointed out in *C.C.C. v. Boulder:*

> Some form of permission from the government must, by necessity, precede such disruptive use of the public domain. We do not see how it could be otherwise. A city needs control over the number of times its citizens must bear the inconvenience of having its streets dug up and the best times for it to occur. Thus, government and cable operators are tied in a way that government and newspapers are not.[60]

But does this tie cable to government so closely that the state may impose restrictions beyond those necessary to assure the peace and safety of its citizens using streets and thoroughfares during construction? Does the First Amendment doctrine permitting the equitable application of business laws to newspapers permit the control of the content of those papers or give government authority to license magazines? In the realm of the First Amendment it has long been decided that a government restriction may be no greater than is necessary to meet the immediate and well-defined state objective.[61] As the Supreme Court noted in *Cantwell v. Connecticut* in 1940:

> When clear and present danger of riot, disorder, interference with traffic upon the streets, or other immediate threat to public safety, peace or order appears, the power of the state to prevent or punish is obvious. Equally obvious is that a State may not unduly suppress free communication of views, religious or other, under the guise of conserving desirable conditions.[62]

To extend the broad control associated with the broadcast model to cable television on the grounds that operators must pass over or under public thoroughfares seems to stretch the rationale beyond its logical capacity. As the appeals court noted in *Preferred*, fairness, access, and indecency controls predicated upon street usage appear infirm at best.[63]

A potentially stronger special circumstance with which to justify application of the broadcast model to cable is the so-called impact rationale generally associated with the notion of the ubiquity and accessibility of the television medium. Unlike both the scarcity and fiduciary models of regulation, this approach is not dependent upon the method of signal transmission; it draws its life from the result of the particular form of communication and, therefore, is equally germane to cable and over-the-air TV.

This concern can be traced as far back as 1952 when the Supreme Court noted the possibility of an alleged "capacity for evil" in the film medium,[64] and may have reached its apex in television in the high court's 1978 decision in *F.C.C. v. Pacifica Foundation,* in which Justice Stevens expressed great concern about radio's social impact and its accessibility to children.[65] The principal difficulty with this argument—in application to either cable or broadcast—is the lack of sound empirical evidence about the nature of television influence. Concern over, and research about, the effects of television are as old as television itself. Despite this fact, scholarly literature remains unsettled with only preliminary findings as to both the long-term and short-term effects of television. Furthermore, the assumed effects attached to broadcast television may not reflect the different case of the more specialized medium prophesied for cable. If ubiquity of television content—the inundating of America with popular television culture—is the concern of the courts, then cable may not fit the associated regulatory framework. A mass audience is not always the goal of cable. Specialized, targeted market segments are the aim of many in cable advertising, and such fractionalization of audience could reduce the validity of the mass audience perspective. But like broad generalizations concerning the impact of broadcast TV, discussion of the impact of fractionalization are mere speculation. In fact, the entire area of effects problems is quite complex and not easily given to hasty conclusions. To erect legal precedent on this ectoplasmic foundation is to fashion law out of mere supposition.

Beyond this questionable empirical foundation is the potentially more important philosophical question of the desirability of restricting speech on the basis of its potential for influence. The question seems to run counter to the intent of almost any reading of the First Amendment. The goal of most political speech is persuasion, and the strength and rightness of the speech is often measured in its ability to alter opinions and behavior; this goes quickly to the heart of the marketplace of ideas. As Emerson has pointed out in his criticism of the "clear and present danger" test:

> To permit the state to cut off expression as soon as it comes close to being effective is essentially to allow only abstract or innocuous expression. . . .

a legal formula framed solely in terms of effectiveness of the expression in influencing action is incompatible with the existence of free expression.[66]

In summary, to restrict communication on the grounds of a presumed potential for influence may be to run directly counter to the philosophy of the First Amendment. Its use as a rationale for broadcast regulation is problematic; its use in cable regulation is suspect.

As to the finer point of *Pacifica,* the availability of broadcast material to children, three things must be said. First, the holding there was a narrow one and should not be construed to provide regulatory justification beyond the facts of the case; even the FCC has admitted as much.[67] Equal time and access regulation certainly cannot be premised on these grounds.

Second, as illustrated by the decision in *Wilkinson,* the use of a print model here would result in the valid rejection of such a rule on the basis of *Butler v. Michigan,* since the issue of the appropriate nature of material for children, by itself, is insufficient legal grounds for the control of either content in general or content specific to the situation.

Third, as pointed out by the court in *Cruz v. Ferre,* the availability of lockboxes under parental control may explode the basis of the argument by eliminating the easy accessibility of the medium to children. Even in this limited context, the argument has flaws.

The final rationale for regulation is, in historical terms, the first. The FCC has urged acceptance, and the courts have accepted, the notion of statutory jurisdiction over cable through its relationship with broadcast television. Most of the analysis of this doctrine has focused on the question of ancillarity, and the degree to which cable in all its specific functions is ancillary to over-the-air TV. Thus, the Supreme Court rejected the commission's attempt in *Midwest Video II* to require cablecasters to provide access, deciding, in part, on the grounds that such a rule was not reasonably ancillary to its authority over broadcasting.[68] But analysis that focuses on the ancillarity doctrine in consideration of the constitutionality of the FCC's authority over cable is misplaced. The special circumstance that appears to provide the window for application of affirmative rights here is not cable's ancillary relation to broadcasting, it is section 153(a) of the Communications Act, which gives the FCC authority over "all interstate and foreign communications by wire or radio",[69] including all "instrumentalities, facilities, apparatus and services [among other things, the receipt, forwarding, and delivery of communications] incidental to such transmission."[70]

Ancillarity only establishes the outer limits of commission authority over cable; it does not provide for that authority in the first instance. That accrues through application of Section 153. The question, then, is the validity of that interpretation, from the Supreme Court's decision in *U.S. v. Southwestern,* in light of the First Amendment. Is the Interstate Communication clause of sufficient weight to overpower the nonutilitarian rights of the cablecaster?

Like the appeals court in *C.C.C. v. Boulder,* which suggests the legitimacy of cable regulation on the grounds that cable has always been regulated, reliance on section 153 to counter constitutional concerns begs the question. There is no doubt that Congress and, perhaps, the FCC have the power to control those portions of the business of cable communication that deal directly with its activity as a business enterprise. Such authority does not, however, give government the right to use such regulations to fashion content agreeable to the aims of the state. Section 153, when invoked as a justification for content control, must itself be questioned on First Amendment grounds. Without additional support, such as a scarcity argument, it could not be used to supplant First Amendment's guarantees. And if application of section 153 cannot meet a constitutional challenge, then validity of the ancillarity doctrine becomes a moot question.

In short, ancillarity has never been used as an original source of justification in cable regulation; it has only set the outer limits of authority legitimated through the use of Section 153, and the constitutional validity of such authority is highly questionable.

Summary

The broadcast model, while the earliest and most heavily invoked model for cable First Amendment rights, suffers two serious drawbacks. With respect to the provision of a model that balances carefully to assure the rights of both the collective and the individual, this approach fails to provide sufficient protection to the individual from potential state interference in free speech rights. It casts the balance too far in favor of the utilitarian supremacy end of the continuum. Practically, the model fails to provide the special circumstance needed to justify the application of the less well-established rights of the collective. The model offers no rationale for the intervention of the state into the First Amendment rights of the cable operator and, therefore, fails to provide for the valid First Amendment interests of the utilitarian goals archetype.

It falls to other models, perhaps, to offer such a balance. The next candidate for consideration is the print model.

Notes

1. 395 U.S. 367, 390 (1969).
2. 412 U.S. 94, 124 (1973).

3. Burger, in fact, quotes Meiklejohn in this case to the effect that "what is essential is not that everyone shall speak but that everything worth saying shall be said." 412 U.S. at 122.

4. 453 U.S. 367, 395 (1981).

5. 47 U.S.C. sec. 301 (1962).

6. 436 U.S. 775, 800 (1978).

7. 47 C.F.R. secs. 76.11 (1977) and 76.12–17 (1982).

8. 47 C.F.R. sec 76.13(c) (1977).

9. 47 C.F.R. sec. 76.31 (1982); *but see Whitehurst v. Grimes*, 21 F.2d 787 (D.C. Ky. 1927) (holding municipal ordinances imposing license requirements on radio broadcasters invalid).

10. *E.g.*, 47 U.S.C. 310 (1982) (forbidding license grants to foreigners); 69 F.C.C.2d 407 (1978) and 72 F.C.C.2d 784 (1979) (establishing financial requirements for applicants).

11. 47 U.S.C. sec. 310(e) (1985).

12. *E.g.*, 47 C.F.R. sec. 73.606 (1982).

13. *National Citizens Committee for Broadcasting v. F.C.C.*, 559 F.2d 187 (D.C. Cir. 1977), *aff'd* 436 U.S. 775 (1978). (upholding broadcast and newspaper cross ownership rules).

14. 47 C.F.R. sec. 76.31(1) (1982).

15. *See*, M. Hamburg, *All About Cable* 4–24(f) (N.Y. Law Journal Seminar-Press, 1981).

16. *E.g.*, 47 C.F.R. sec. 76.501 (1985).

17. 33 Fed. Reg. 28 (1968).

18. *But see*, N.Y. Exec. Law sec. 815(2)(b); Minn. Stat. Ann. sec. 238.05(2)(b).

19. *C.B.S. v. D.N.C.*, 412 U.S. 94 (1973) and *F.C.C. v. Midwest Video*, 440 U.S. 689 (1979).

20. 47 U.S.C. sec. 312(a)(7) (1985).

21. 47 C.F.R. sec. 73.1920 (1982).

22. 47 C.F.R. secs. 76.205, 76.209 (1982).

23. *C.B.S. v. D.N.C.*

24. 47 C.F.R. secs. 73.1720, 73.1725 (1982).

25. *E.g.*, *N.B.C. v. United States*, 319 U.S. 190 (1943).

26. *E.g.*, *RKO General v. F.C.C.*, 670 F.2d 215 (1981).

27. 47 C.F.R. secs. 73.1800–1840 (1985).

28. 47 C.F.R. sec. 73.2080 (1982).

29. 47 C.F.R. sec. 76.305 (1982).

30. 47 C.F.R. sec. 76.311 (1982).

31. 47 C.F.R. sec. 76.501 (1985).

32. 47 C.F.R. sec. 76.605 (1985).

33. *E.g.*, Del. Code Ann. tit. 26, sec. 602(g) (1980), and N.Y. Exec. Law sec. 815(2)(c)(ii) (1982).

34. *E.g.*, Mass. Gen. Laws Ann. ch. 166A, sec. 5(a) (1982), and Haw. Rev. Stat. sec. 440G6(b)(1) (1982).

35. *E.g.*, N.Y. Exec. Law secs. 823, 815(2)(d)(iv) (1982), and Minn. Stat. Ann. sec. sec. 238.05(12), 238.05(6) (1982).

36. *E.g.,* N.Y. Exec. Law. sec. 825(1)(4) (1982), Minn. Stat. Ann. sec. 238.10, (1982), and Mass. Gen. Laws. Ann. ch. 166A, sec. 15 (1982).

37. 436 F.2d 263 (1970).

38. 506 F.2d 246 (1974).

39. *F.C.C. v. WNCN Listeners Guild,* 450 U.S. 582 (1981).

40. *Id.* at 603.

41. Report and Statement of Policy in Re: Commission en banc Programming Inquiry, 44 F.C.C. 2303 (1960).

42. Rules governing applicability of the Fairness Doctrine, personal attack, and political editorials remain in effect for cable operator origination (47 C.F.R. sec. 76.209) despite a 1981 FCC staff report critical of the rules ("Cable Television and the Political Broadcasting Laws: The 1980 Election Experience and Proposals for Change," Cable Television Bureau, F.C.C., January 1981).

43. 47 C.F.R. sec. 73.1212 (1985).

44. 47 C.F.R. sec. 73.4075 (1985).

45. 44 F.C.C.2d 1016 (1974).

46. 26 F.C.C.2d 275 (1970).

47. *Banzhaf v. F.C.C.,* 405 F.2d 1082 (D.C. Cir. 1968).

48. *National Citizens Committee v. F.C.C.,* 567 F.2d 1095 (D.C. Cir. 1977).

49. 15 U.S.C. sec. 1335 (1982).

50. *Capital Broadcasting Co. v. Mitchell,* 333 F. Supp. 582, 584 (D. D.C. 1971).

51. 333 F. Supp. at 585.

52. R. Sadowski, "Broadcasters and State Statutory Laws," 18 *J. of Broadcasting* 433 (1974).

53. 24 F.C.C. 2d 408 (1970).

54. *Yale Broadcasting v. F.C.C.,* 478 F.2d 594 (D.C. Cir. 1973) *cert. denied,* 414 U.S. 914 (1973) (upholding the FCC's authority to pressure broadcasters to guard against playing drug-related music).

55. SB 6100 (1982).

56. 47 U.S.C. sec. 326 (1962).

57. *E.g., Greater Freemont v. City of Freemont,* 302 F.Supp. 652, 657 (N.D. Ohio 1968), and *C.C.C. v. Boulder,* 485 F.Supp 1035 (D. Colo. 1980).

58. *See, e.g.,* R. Hochberg, *The States Regulate Cable,* at 28 (Cambridge, MA: Harvard University, 1978).

59. *See e.g.,* F.C.C. Staff Report on Cable TV Cross Ownership Policies, 97 n.28 (Nov. 27, 1981), or Dawson, *How Safe is Cable's Natural Monopoly?* Cablevision, June 1, 1981, at 333.

60. 660 F.2d at 1377–78.

61. *See Lovell v. Griffin,* 303 U.S. 444 (1938) and *Cantwell v. Connecticut,* 310 U.S. 296 (1949).

62. 310 U.S. at 308.

63. *See Preferred,* at 15–18, and *C.C.C. v. Boulder,* 630 F.2d 704 (1980) (Markey, J., dissenting).

64. *Burstyn v. Wilson,* 343 U.S. 495, 502 (1952).

65. 438 U.S. 726, 756–61 (1978).

66. T. Emerson, *Toward a General Theory of the First Amendment*, 52 (NY: Random House, 1966).

67. *See, In re* WGBH Educational Foundation, F.C.C., 69 F.C.C.2d 1250, 1254 (1978).

68. 440 U.S. 689, 708 (1979).

69. 47 U.S.C. sec. 152(a) (1962).

70. 47 U.S.C. sec. 153(b) (1962).

7
The Print Model

R iding the wave of deregulation, the cable industry in the late 1970s and early 1980s began lobbying strenuously for the approval of new regulatory and constitutional laws for cable. The First Amendment should apply no differently to cable than it does to newspapers, declared National Cable Television Association lawyers:

> Cable operators are entitled to the freedom of speech granted newspapers, without conditions and without requirements of access or balance. . . . to deny First Amendment rights to cable operators, is to undermine not merely cable's constitutional rights, but society's interest in diverse expressions of points of view.[1]

What would a print model of First Amendment rights for cable look like? And what justification might there be for such an application? This chapter considers the problems and promises of a print model of cable rights.

The print model—as defined here—represents the classic assumptions about the purposes and goals of the First Amendment. As suggested in chapter 5, the print model draws its strength from a combination of both the nonutilitarian and utilitarian consequences positions on the social utility continuum. Government is prevented from inhibiting the speech of the individual because of both the inherent value of self-expression in such activity and the good that would flow to the state as a result of such protection.

It is from this libertarian foundation that the Supreme Court has found reason to consistently strike down laws aimed at silencing the individual speaker,[2] the pamphleteer,[3] the picketer,[4] the protester,[5] the crusading newspaper,[6] and even the modern corporation.[7] However, this model is distinguished by its inherent inability to provide a special constitutional protection for designated social institutions such as the press and by its inability to break down nongovernmental barriers to the free flow of information.

The dualistic schema of both Brennan and Stewart illustrate this schism. Their speech models of the First Amendment extend protection to all who invoke it and, thereby, rests on a classic libertarian foundation. Their structural models hold out special privileges, such as the right to gather information, to the news media on the basis of the press's special status as an institution in service to the people's right to know. No such extraordinary powers flow from the nonutilitarian end of the social utility continuum. More importantly, for purposes of this discussion, the print model does not suggest a special ability of the government to inject itself into the private sector for the purposes of facilitating expressive activities in the name of the good of society. As the Supreme Court stated in *Hudgens v. N.L.R.B.*:

> It is, of course, a commonplace that the Constitutional guarantee of free speech is a guarantee only against abridgment by government, federal or state. Thus, while statutory or common law may in some situations extend protection or provide redress against a private corporation or person who seeks to abridge the free expression of others, no such protection or redress is provided by the Constitution itself.[8]

The model, therefore, addresses only the permissible limits of government restriction on speech. It need never concern itself about special circumstances that might justify the intervention of the government to promote expression, for it rejects the premise of such power. The First Amendment, under this interpretation, is solely and exclusively a restraint on government. It assumes a smoothly functioning marketplace which would only suffer as a result of government interference.

Application of the Model

There are, of course, limits and exceptions to the barrier between government and communicator under this model. The regulation and control of communications industries, including cable, is permitted within certain boundaries. But cable, under the print model, would assume a very different set of legal protections and restrictions than it operates under today in terms of its structure, behavior, and content.

Structure

In the first instance, it would be constitutionally impermissible to require the licensing of cable systems by federal, state, or local government. If little else is clear from the Supreme Court's interpretation of the First Amendment it is that government may not mandate prior approval for the dissemination of constitutionally protected expression. As the court pointed out in *Lovell v. Griffin*:

The struggle for freedom of the press was primarily directed against the power of the licensor. . . . While this freedom from previous restraint upon publication cannot be regarded as exhausting the guarantee of liberty, the prevention of that restraint was a leading purpose in the adoption of the constitutional provision.[9]

The FCC's now defunct certificate of compliance, therefore, would have been unconstitutional under this model,[10] and the very nature of franchising as it now exists would, quite probably, be unconstitutional as well. A city would maintain the ability to regulate a variety of aspects of the business of cable television, but any general license to disseminate information in the community, extending beyond a content-neutral time, place, and manner ordinance, would certainly fall outside the acceptable limits of the First Amendment. (This, as noted previously, may be the direction in which the courts are headed).

Since the First Amendment interests of the collective, as expressed through statutes and ordinances aimed at controlling the structure of the industry, would have to give way to the superior First Amendment rights of the owner-operator, the many other types of structural controls now associated with the broadcast model would be forbidden. For example, as licensing in general would be unconstitutional, so would all constraints on the length of time an individual could run a system and constraints on the nature and background of the owner. That is, the sort of character, financial, and technical requirements codified in FCC regulations and most municipal franchise proposals would have to be abandoned. Furthermore, the multiple ownership regulations applied to broadcasters[11] and once considered for cable operators would be unconstitutional as well.

Structural controls would be relegated to the status of laws as they apply to the newspaper industry. The continued prohibition on network ownership of cable would be supportable through application of cross-ownership regulation preventing the holders of television licenses, in certain situations, from owning cable outlets.[12] Where the courts have upheld the FCC's right to bar cross-ownership of newspapers and broadcast outlets in the same town,[13] similar restrictions on broadcast and cable would be applicable to cable. But laws attempting to prevent cross-ownership of newspapers and cable[14] could not be constitutionally justified.

Antitrust laws, while formally applicable, would probably run into problems similar to those experienced in the newspaper business, where the nature of the economic structure of the industry militates against effective use of either the Sherman or Clayton Antitrust Acts to break down monopoly situations.[15] The major problem here is that while antitrust laws can be used to attack monopolies formed as a result of anticompetitive practices[16] or to restrict companies shown to be using their dominant market position as leverage in maintaining monopoly control,[17] the laws are not easily applied to so-called natural monopolies—monopolies that are thrust upon a company as the result of natural market forces.[18]

The ownership patterns of the industry, in short, would be relatively free from constraints either in the form of antitrust laws or regulatory limitations. Pure economic forces would dictate industry structure just as they do in the newspaper sector.

As previously noted, the applicability of access control to cable under the broadcast model is problematic. No such ambiguity arises under the print model. The inviolability of the newspaper's editorial pages no longer seems to be an issue. As early as 1933, the Iowa Supreme Court, in a case involving the question of a newspaper's right to accept or reject advertising, ruled that a newspaper was a private enterprise and its management had no duty to be a public utility that served everyone who came along.[19] Similarly, in 1970 a federal appellate court turned down a labor union's appeal for access to the advertising columns of the *Chicago Tribune*.[20] And a 1971 appellate court ruling held that newspapers had no obligation to run movie advertisements.[21] Finally, with the *Tornillo* decision in 1974, the Supreme Court appeared to foreclose, at least for the near future, the possibility of arguing for editorial access. Economic monopoly is, therefore, insufficient to overcome the strong constitutional protection of the editor-publisher, and by extension, it would be insufficient under a print model to overcome the prerogatives of the cable operator-editor. As the court stated in *Tornillo:*

> The choice of material to go into a newspaper, and the decisions made as to the limitations on size of the paper, and content, and treatment of public issues and public officials—whether fair or unfair—constitutes the exercise of editorial control and judgment. It has yet to be demonstrated how government regulation of this crucial process can be exercised consistent with First Amendment guarantees of a free press as they have evolved at this time.[22]

Access channels, like the op-ed pages of a newspaper, would be provided and controlled only at the discretion of the cable operator. While the operator might find it economically and politically attractive to provide such a service to the community or the government and the educational system of the area, such channels could not be required by any level of government. Such a situation would follow more closely the decision of the appeals court in *Midwest Video II*, extending the First Amendment logic of that decision to the state and local levels.

The panoply of access and ownership requirements currently and historically part of cable regulation would, therefore, under a print model of regulation, be demolished. The market would rule the structure of the industry.

Behavior

While the laws normally applicable to other businesses are equally applicable to communications industries such as newspapers and cablecasting, inequitable regulations, or regulations which go beyond those traditionally associated with legitimate business regulation for the purpose of controlling or intimidating expression, have been found in violation of the First Amendment.[23] The legitimacy of business taxes on newspapers, therefore, is generally without controversy,[24] but when those taxes are formulated to punish, intimidate, or benefit the media, they violate the constitution.[25] Similarly, there is no special First Amendment protection from labor laws[26] unless those laws infringe directly upon freedom of expression.[27] As a result, the state, under the print model, may constitutionally regulate many of the aspects of the routine of the daily dissemination of information as long as those rules are sharply confined to such issues as might be equally applicable to other economic endeavors: the distribution of material in accordance with local safety, noise, or littering ordinances, for example.[28] And such restrictions are forbidden only when they turn on the nature of the content,[29] are constitutionally overbroad or vague,[30] or act to prohibit material entirely.[31]

In short, the taxation and regulation of cable television under the print model would be permissible within the bounds established by a long line of speech and press cases. As noted in the previous chapter, there appear to be no constitutional barriers to regulations regarding the safe stringing or laying of wire across city streets and parkways, nor does logic dictate there should be. Regulations regarding pole attachment and easement for right of way are common and pose no First Amendment question as long as they are administered with an eye toward constitutional exactitude.

At the same time, significant federal controls on nontechnical behavior—Equal Employment oversight and community ascertainment guidelines—could run afoul of the First Amendment. Community ascertainment, as it was tied to programming considerations, is particularly suspect. Maintenance of program logs and annual financial reporting might also fall to overriding constitutional concerns.

The single most important behavioral control at the local level is the establishment of cable rate structures in the public interest. With print model protection, the authority of local government to oversee this area of cable operation is highly problematic. Little precedent exists here, but at least one cable company has directly challenged the authority of the state to regulate user rates. In 1980 Cape Cod Cablevision Corporation filed suit against the Massachusetts Cable Television Commission in order to prevent that body from implementing rate regulation rules.[32] The company claimed that such regulations violated the company's First Amendment right to be insulated from government regulations that might affect the editorial discretion of the communicator. The company further pointed out that such a law placed the financial health of the company in the hands of policy makers who might otherwise be subject to coverage and even criticism by the cable company. This presented a strong chilling effect on First Amendment rights, according to the company.[33] While there was no subsequent adjudication in the case, it does illustrate the problem and point to potential grounds for the future challenge of such regulations.

In short, any behavioral controls that went beyond laws generally associated with the legitimate regulation of business activities, especially if they affected content, would be impermissible.

Content

All constitutionally accepted control of communicative content—such as obscenity, libel, and privacy—would attach to cable as they attach to all media under the print model of First Amendment rights. No special privileges are implied under this form of cable regulation.

Controls beyond these well-defined parameters would not survive First Amendment scrutiny, however. Absent a showing of clear and present danger or a demonstration that the material in question fell outside the reach of the First Amendment (i.e., obscenity), the federal, state, and local authorities would be forbidden from limiting through statute or enforced contract the substantive nature of the cablecaster's programming. Control of programming would be considered an editorial function, insulated from government tampering. While such autonomy would be more pronounced in political programming than in programming of a strictly entertainment or commercial nature, it would, nonetheless, be superior to most forms of protection afforded broadcasters. Hence, the multitude of content controls historically and currently associated with cable television would have to fall.

The former, but long-time, regulations restricting the importation and retransmission of distant signals would seem to come under this category of unconstitutional content controls. Given adherence by cablecasters to the appropriate copyright regulations governing retransmission, even Congress would be restricted in its ability to limit carriage.

The restrictions on political broadcasting—Fairness Doctrine and Equal Time—also would be prohibited with the application of a print model. The existing federal laws applying these restrictions to local origination channels would be eliminated, as would any attempts to apply similar controls at the state and local levels.

Quincy already has demonstrated that the "must carry" rules requiring carriage of specific local stations must succumb to a First Amendment attack using the print model, in part on the grounds that such control could amount to compelled speech. According to the D.C. Circuit:

The difficulty is not so much that the rules force operators to act as a mouthpiece for ideological perspectives they do not share, although such a result is by no means implausible. The more certain injury stems from the substantial limitations the rules work on the operator's otherwise broad discretion to select the programming it offers subscribers.[34]

While such rules do not constitute the enforced dissemination of a specific political ideology,[35] the general state directive of carriage might find parallels in cases that do. As the Supreme Court noted in *Wooley v. Maynard,* "We begin with the proposition that the right of freedom of thought protected by the First Amendment against state action includes both the right to speak freely and the right to refrain from speaking at all."[36]

Finally, the holding of the district court in *H.B.O. v. Wilkinson* would presumably represent the typical print model position with respect to the cablecasting of so-called indecent speech. Within the limits of *Miller,* states could not constitutionally abridge the rights of cablecasters to program X or R rated movies, or any other sexually oriented materials they chose.

On the other hand, and interestingly enough, application of a print model of protection would strip cable companies of much of the state-supplied insulation from liability they've enjoyed as a result of mandated access. Total protection from government interference in the programming function would imply total responsibility for programming content; cable companies would be legally liable for any infraction of existing applicable laws pertaining to content. Legislatures certainly would be within their authority to extend special protection from private and state legal action if they wished, just as they enact news reporter shield laws, but without the rationale of an associated access of origination requirement, there would seem little motivation for such action.

A print model of cable regulation would, therefore, establish a free enterprise system of cablecasting in which operators would compete as they wished for local customers without the necessity of securing a local license to do so. Rates charged would be established on the basis of that free market competition without state or local floors or ceilings. Franchise fees would be eliminated along with the franchises, and cable systems would be subject only to the normal business taxes associated with any enterprise. Access channels would be offered only to the extent that cable operators wished to extend them, with such a decision presumably based on economic and public relations grounds, not legal grounds. The programming of all channels, its substance, scheduling, and cost, would be determined by the owner with due respect for libel, obscenity, and commercial speech considerations, and guided by consumer preference. Cable customers dissatisfied with existing or proposed service, rates, or programming would be free to seek the service of a competitor if one were available, decline the service if one were not, or, given sufficient desire and resources, initiate a new, competing cable service. Such a scenario, while seemingly far removed from present and even potential reality, appears the aim of the cable industry and the goal toward which it is working. The next question for consideration here is the practical and philosophical merit of this model.

Critique

The need for special circumstances in which to assert an affirmative role for the service of the collective is, as previously noted, not a question here. There is no presumption of the need to serve the collective interest; the philosophical origins and the goals of the model dictate only that the state keep out of the free speech affairs of the individual. When this course is followed, the collective will be served in its own good way. The consequence for the print model, as considered here, is the total lack of practical problem in its invocation and use in cable regulation. That is, there are no First Amendment barriers to the application of the model to cable. This, of course, has been the thrust of several court decisions, *Quincy* and the appellate ruling in *Preferred* being the most influential. The absence of First Amendment barriers does not suggest that application of the print model to cable best serves the interests of an equitable protection theory of First Amendment rights.

While the lack of a need for special circumstances appears to be the principal practical strength of the print model, it is, at the same time, its fundamental philosophical weakness. The model rests on a commitment to the rights of the individual and, to some extent, the belief that the results of such protection will benefit the whole. This second point is important for it suggests that at least one aspect of the print model draws strength from the middle range of the social utility continuum that holds service to the collective to be an important social value. And scholars and philosophers who hold to a libertarian line often fall back on the alleged efficacy of this trickle-down theory of First Amendment rights. The print model does not argue against the value or necessity of collectivistic free speech arguments, it only differs in the method of such service.

The position here, however, is that the print model is, in application to cable, untenable because the assumptions of the trickle-down theory are not met. With respect at least to cable, Baker's failed market theory is the most relevant framework for analysis. In the newspaper industry, the assumptions of diversity within the marketplace, and ease of entry into the arena of expression, have, according to critics such as Barron, been lost over time through the economic realities of a capital economy.[37] But to the extent that the assumptions of the print model have eroded in the newspaper industry, they probably never even existed in the cable industry. As has been repeatedly pointed out by the courts, economists, and the industry itself, the business of cable television appears to be a natural economic monopoly. A single owner-operator, a lone communications company, will most likely control a given geographic area to the exclusion of all potential competitors. Recently, proponents of deregulation have begun to dispute cable's status as a natural economic monopoly, invoking two lines of argument: first, that there is no substantial documentation that economic forces will tend to create a monopoly situation for cable in a given market, and second, that competing information technologies will restrict cable's ability to levy monopolistic charges.[38]

There is little empirical support for the first argument. All the major independent studies have shown cable to exhibit, to a greater or lesser degree, a declining average cost curve similar to that in the daily newspaper industry.[39] This is the primary characteristic of a natural economic monopoly. It suggests that, over time, one firm will come to monopolize a given market. Beyond the econometric evidence is the substantiation of real life. There are more than 6,000 cable systems operating in the United States and fewer than twenty have ever competed head-to-head at a given time.[40] Further, the laws of economics suggest that situations in which competition does exist will eventually resolve themselves in the elimination of one of the competing firms. This tendency toward monopoly is generally not disputed in its existence, only in its strength. Those who argue against government regulation of the industry cite reports that suggest the economies "are not so large as to rule out the possibility of competition."[41] But this is a rather weak modifier to the general observation that such economies do operate, and it is of little interest to the ninety-nine percent of current cable systems which do exist as monopolies. Arguments that deregulation of cable will result in a grand surge of industry competition fly in the face of reality.

As to whether cable systems are able to exact monopolistic charges, two things must be noted. First, the extent to which cable companies can use their monopoly position to manipulate basic cable subscriber rates is as yet unclear. For most of cable's history, the majority of the country's systems have been regulated by state and local government, and the natural pricing mechanism for basic services has been unable to operate. Some argue that the competition from other, new television technologies such as multipoint distribution services, low power TV, and direct broadcast satellite will prevent the exercise of monopolistic pricing by cable firms.[42] This question is not settled, however, because most of these potential competitors are still in an embryonic stage of development and not yet a tangible economic force. (Direct broadcast satellites, for example, have yet to show any sign of becoming a part of domestic communications in the near future.) In one of the more recent studies of cable pricing structures, economists concluded that "no substitute beside broadcast television measurably influences the demand for basic and pay cable."[43] Of course, many areas of the country served by cable still lack access to a variety of over-the-air television signals, eliminating even that source of potential competition. In short, the power of unregulated cable systems to charge monopolistic prices is yet to be determined.

More importantly for present purposes, the issue itself lacks substantial relevance. The concern here is not with pricing but with the appropriate First Amendment model and the related concern of monopolizing a given means of communication. As pointed out in the opening chapter, the Supreme Court has rejected arguments that all media forms should be governed by one set of constitutional principles. For First Amendment purposes cable must be treated as an independent medium and all evidence points to the conclusion that, in most cases and in most areas, that medium is going to hold a monopoly position.

Therefore, although the courts have ruled that the presence of economic monopoly alone is insufficient to override the constitutional protection provided the communicator under the print model, the absolute control a communicator has over the free flow of ideas through that particular medium within that particular area is no less real; and the danger to the collective is equally real. Social, cultural, and political ideas and opinions at odds with the owner of a monopolistic communications system face the possibility of never reaching the audience for which they were intended. The collective is denied the interchange of thought that powers the polity. The First Amendment rights espoused by Meiklejohn are frustrated, and even the utilitarian consequences approach to First Amendment rights endangered.

With respect to the broad aims outlined in chapter 5, the print model, when applied to cable television regulation, appears to fall short. While the model may, in fact, work effectively for some media, the peculiar characteristics of cable are such that the major assumptions of the model cannot be met. The essential mechanism of an open economic marketplace, at least in this medium, does not appear to be a realizable achievement. The print model, therefore, while eminently practical, must be rejected on philosophical grounds. It simply fails to meet the criteria for an equitable protection model of First Amendment rights.

Notes

1. B. Ross, "The First Amendment: A New Interpretation Needed for Cable," *Cablevision*, May 18, 1981, at 156.

2. *E.g., Thomas v. Collins,* 323 U.S. 516 (1945).

3. *E.g., Lovell v. Griffin,* 303 U.S. 444 (1938).

4. *E.g., Thornhill v. Alabama,* 310 U.S. 88 (1940).

5. *E.g., Cohen v. California,* 403 U.S. 15 (1971).

6. *E.g., Near v. Minnesota*, 283 U.S. 697 (1931).

7. *First National Bank of Boston v. Bellotti*, 435 U.S. 765 (1978).

8. 424 U.S. 507, 513 (1976).

9. 303 U.S. at 451–52.

10. 47 C.F.R. sec. 76.11 (1977).

11. 47 U.S.C. 73.3555 (1985).

12. 47 C.F.R. 76.501 (1980).

13. *F.C.C. v. N.C.C.B.*, 436 U.S. 775 (1978).

14. *E.g.*, Mass. Gen. Laws Ann., ch. 166A, sec. 5(j) (1979).

15. *See* G. Jones, "Antitrust Malaise in the Newspaper Industry: The Chains Continue To Grow," 8 *St. Mary's L. J.* 160 (1976).

16. *See Lorain Journal v. United States*, 342 U.S. 143 (1951), and *Mansfield Journal v. F.C.C.*, 180 F.2d 28 (1950).

17. *United States v. AlCoa*, 148 F.2d 416 (1945).

18. *United States v. U.S. Steel Corp.*, 251 U.S. 417, 451 (1920).

19. *Shuck v. Carroll Daily Herald*, 247 N.W. 813 (1933).

20. *Chicago Joint Board, Amalgamated Clothing Workers of America v. Chicago Tribune*, 435 F.2d 470 (1970).

21. *Associates and Aldrich v. Times Mirror*, 440 F.2d 133 (1971).

22. 418 U.S. 241, 258 (1974).

23. *Grosjean v. American Press*, 297 U.S. 233 (1936).

24. *See e.g. City of Corona v. Corona Daily Independent*, 115 Cal. App.2d 382 (1953).

25. *Minneapolis Star and Tribune v. Minnesota Commissioner of Revenue*, 460 U.S. 575 (1983).

26. *A.P. v. N.L.R.B.*, 301 U.S. 103 (1937).

27. *Evans v. American Federation of Television and Radio Artists*, 354 F.Supp. 823 (S.D.N.Y., 1973).

28. *See e.g. Cox v. New Hampshire*, 312 U.S. 569 (1941) (upholding parade permits); *Kovacs v. Cooper*, 336 U.S. 77 (1949) (upholding restrictions on sound trucks); *Socialist Labor Party v. Glendale*, 82 Cal. App. 3d 722 (1978) (upholding tightly drawn ordinances controlling newsracks).

29. *Schad v. Mt. Ephram*, 452 U.S. 61 (1981) (striking down a zoning ordinance banning nude dancing).

30. *Cantwell v. Connecticut*, 310 U.S. 296 (1949).

31. *Philadelphia News, Inc. v. Borough C. Etc., Swathmore*, 381 F. Supp 228 (1974) (involving a ban on newsracks on city streets entirely).

32. *Cape Cod Cable Television Corp. v. Community Antenna Television Commission and the Commonwealth of Massachusetts*, Superior Court of Suffolk County, Mass., Civil Action No. 44121 (1980).

33. *Id.*

34. *Quincy Cable Television v. F.C.C.*, 768 F.2d 1434, 1452 (D.C. Cir. 1985).

35. *See Wooley v. Maynard*, 430 U.S. 705 (1977).

36. 430 U.S. at 714.

37. J. Barron, *Freedom of the Press for Whom?*, 4–5 (Bloomington, IN: Indiana University Press, 1975).

38. *See e.g.,* G. Shapiro, P. Kurland and J. Mercurio, *CableSpeech: The Case for First Amendment Protection,* 8–13 (New York: Harcourt Brace Jovanovich, 1983).

39. *See e.g.,* G.K. Webb, *The Economics of Cable Television* (Lexington, MA: Lexington Books, 1983); S.M. Bensen, B.M. Mitchell, R.G. Noll, B.M. Owen, R.E. Park, and J.N. Rosse, *Economic Policy Research on Cable Television: Assessing the Costs and Benefits of Cable Deregulation* (Washington D.C.: Office of Telecommunications Policy, 1976); M. Seiden, "An Economic Analysis of Community Antenna Television Systems and the Television Broadcasting Industry," reprinted in *Progress Report from FCC-1965, Hearings Before the Subcomm. on Communication of the Senate Comm. on Commerce,* 89th Cong., 1st Sess. (1965); Noam, "Is Cable Television a Natural Monopoly?" Research Working Paper #430A, Columbia University (Feb. 1982); B.M. Owen and P.R. Greenhalgh, "Competitive Policy Considerations in Cable Television Franchising," reprinted in *Options for Cable Legislation, Hearings Before the Subcomm. on Telecommunications, Consumer Protection and Finance of the House Comm. on Energy and Commerce,* 98th Cong., 1st Sess. (Serial no. 98–73)

40. Shapiro, *supra,* at 12, and Webb, *id.,* at 41.

41. Owen and Greenhalgh, *supra,* at 69.

42. *See e.g.,* Shapiro, *supra,* at 9–10.

43. Webb, *supra,* at 87–88.

8
The Public Forum Model

The broadcast and print models of cable regulation represent traditional, mainstream approaches to the discussion of cable rights. Three nontraditional models that appear in the literature and represent paths to the balancing of individual and collective First Amendment claims, include the public forum, common carrier, and public utility models. This chapter considers the public forum approach.

The question of public access to government-licensed communications systems gives almost immediate rise to the question of public forum theory.[1] As traditionally defined, public forum theory provides nondiscriminatory public access for First Amendment purposes to public places traditionally situated for such activity. The history of public forum theory has been traced back to *Commonwealth v. Davis*[2] in 1895 when the notion of such access was initially rejected.[3] Modern public forum theory begins with *Hague v. C.I.O.* in 1939 in which the Supreme Court reversed the *Davis* opinion, declaring:

> Wherever the title of the streets and parks may rest, they have immemorably been held in trust for the use of the public and, time out of mind, have been used for purposes of assembly, communicating thoughts between citizens and discussing public questions.[4]

Hague drew out of English common law a sort of First Amendment easement, a right to use the public streets and parks for communicative activity.[5] Despite the fact that various restrictions may be placed on the use of public thoroughfares for such activity,[6] the public forum doctrine has been extended to provide coverage for expressive activity in airports,[7] bus terminals,[8] school grounds and auditoriums,[9] public hospitals,[10] the U.S. Capitol grounds, [11] and the Supreme Court grounds.[12] However, reasonable time, place, and manner limits may be placed on the activity.[13]

Application of the Model

Structure and Behavior

The extension of a public forum approach could generate a variety of benefits for cable rights on both sides. In the first instance, government regulation under the model would be severely limited to narrow structural and behavioral controls. The model neither demands, grants, nor implies the validity of general state jurisdiction over every aspect of cable operation. It bestows no authority to set limits on the ownership of cable systems nor, for that matter, requires that an established number of channels be set aside for public access. Neither does the model assume to impose regulations requiring such activities as community ascertainment of needs. And it neither necessitates nor requires for its application the local control over customer rates. It, thereby, leaves a great deal of discretion for the cable operator concerning the organization and management of the business. In this respect, it more closely parallels the print model than the broadcast model.

The only permissible mandate of the public forum model is the proffering by the cable company of sufficient access time and space to satisfy the demand of the community and individuals within the community for necessary expressive activity. It is, in fact, a relatively straightforward access requirement. The important difference between this access requirement and those forged by federal, state, and local authorities is that this requirement is not statutory; it springs from the Constitution, or rather a specific interpretation of the First Amendment rights of the community with respect to the asserted public forum of cable TV. It is, thereby, distinguished from access requirements fashioned from legislative or municipal desire to require access in possible violation of the rights of the cablecaster. This is a particular vision of First Amendment rights that attempts a balance between the rights of the individual cablecaster and the rights of the community.

Content

One advantage of the public forum approach, one which helps insure the unfettered expression of both cablecaster and community, is the safeguards against content-based regulations. As noted, reasonable time, place, and manner controls might be permitted, but even then such controls would need to be content neutral. According to the Supreme Court:

> Once a forum is opened to assembly or speaking by some groups, government may not prohibit others from assembling or speaking on the basis of what they intend to say. Selective exclusions from a public forum may not be based on content alone.[14]

In general, the invocation of a public forum model in cable television would result in a requirement that access be granted to individuals seeking a local outlet for expression, but the state would be forbidden to interfere with the cable operator beyond assuring such access. Special structural and behavioral controls would not be permitted as the result of public forum application, and the First Amendment rights of the cable operator would be protected.

Critique

The public forum model seems to serve admirably the balancing of interests sought in an equitable protection model. It provides for the protection of the rights of the community to receive information and ideas which a cable operator on his or her own might be loath to disseminate, and, at the same time, it prevents government from either censoring the cablecaster or using the model to enact structural or behavioral controls that might chill the cablecaster's speech.

It is, in essence, a social goals approach that admittedly sacrifices some operator control and rights, but does so at a much lower level than the more collectivistically oriented broadcast model. Such a model might be attractive to those seeking a workable compromise between conflicting First Amendment ideals.

Before celebrating the discovery of a workable model, however, the validity of the application of public forum theory to cable television demands close scrutiny. Benefits cannot be derived where the foundational elements for extension of the model are missing.

The legitimacy of applying the public forum model must begin with a consideration of the requisite elements necessary for the establishment of a public forum. These elements include state action, demonstration of traditional use of the area for such activities, and compatibility with the normal usage of the area. In the first instance, it is necessary that the area in question be controlled directly by the government or so closely resemble such control as to make the distinction irrelevant.[15] Secondly, the assumed public forum must have some historically based nexus with the exercise of free speech. Streets and parks, for example, are held in *Hague* and subsequent cases to be "historically associated with the exercise of First Amendment rights."[16] Finally, the courts have suggested that the activity in question should be compatible with the normal usage of the asserted forum. Picketers, therefore, have been subjected to time, place, and manner restraints on the basis of the incompatibility of their activities with the functioning of a nearby school.[17] Normally, it appears that this latter element acts only to delimit the exercise of activities in a public forum rather than destroy a potential finding of the existence of one.

The question of state action, then, represents the first concern in attempting to apply a public forum model to cable. State action exists, by definition, where the government owns and directly controls the claimed forum. Streets, sidewalks, and parks are the most obvious examples. The doctrine has been extended to some communications media when it has been demonstrated that the state has some ownership or controlling interest. Student newspapers in public schools are considered public forums for most purposes.[18] Municipally owned theaters also have been declared public forums by the Supreme Court.[19]

Most cable systems are not, however, owned by the state. They do require an operating license, but any attempt to claim access rights on the basis of municipal or federal licensing is, in a public forum context, quite tautological, since it is the constitutional validity of the licensing itself that is in question. (This is reminiscent of the circular majority argument in the circuit court decision in *C.C.C. v. Boulder* that upheld the validity of local control, in part, on the basis of the long history of local control.) Is is state action itself that is problematic here; the issue is whether there is sufficient state action for the construction of a public forum-based right of access, and the direct answer appears to be no.

A potential solution to the apparent lack of direct state action might be invocation of the notion of indirect state action as applied in the *Marsh* case. There, a company town, owned and operated by a private concern, was declared to have had sufficient governmental functions and attributes to support a finding that state action was present and the town's street could be classified as public forums. This application was briefly extended to shopping centers in *Amalgamated Food Employees Union v. Logan Valley Plaza, Inc.,*[20] when the Supreme Court declared this type of generally private property to be a public forum when the type of speech at issue was directly related to the purpose of property. Given the public nature and monopoly status of most cable systems, such a finding might lead to a limited public forum classification for cable as nearly any requested access would be directly related to the purpose of the system. Unfortunately, this budding doctrine was short-lived, with the high court backing away from it in *Lloyd v. Tanner* in 1972,[21] and completing repudiating it in *Hudgens v. N.L.R.B.* in 1976.[22] In the latter case, Justice Stewart, for the majority, suggested that extending the doctrine simply on the basis of compatible uses was no longer valid, and that private property could not be made into a First Amendment forum on the grounds that the public had been invited for other purposes. Only *Marsh* appeared to be left standing after *Hudgens,* implying that extension of state action to private property would only be upheld in the very narrow circumstances of that case, circumstances that seem inapplicable to cable television.

Still another argued route for the application of state action might be a strict compatibility analysis.[23] For example, in *Southeastern Promotions*, the Supreme Court held out a thread of hope for the extension of public forum doctrine to cable by suggesting the impropriety of government censorship of a forum—a city auditorium—which traditionally had been dedicated to expressive activity. Drawing from this, the function and use of cable systems may be so intertwined with public communication as to make mandated public access compatible with that function. This compatibility analysis might lead to a public forum application. Again, unfortunately, the courts have declined to extend this analysis to communication forums analogous to cable. In situations involving certain student newspapers[24] and public broadcasting stations[25] the courts have declined to find a public forum, suggesting that these media had, inherent in their management, an insular layer of control between government and the public. Government did not have direct control over these media due to this insulation and so state action did not apply. In fact, the media had a strong dose of their own constitutional rights, according to the courts.

In *Mississippi Gay Alliance v. Goudelock* in 1976, for example, a federal appeals court rejected a request for access to the ad columns of the Mississippi State University newspaper by the Mississippi Gay Alliance.[26] The court stated that, unlike previous cases, the staff of the newspaper and not the university administration had rejected the advertising and, therefore, there was no state action.

Similarly, the Supreme Court in *CBS v. DNC* rejected a lower court holding of state action in broadcasting, stating that the intent of the legislation that established the television system was to provide for privately run stations with government oversights.[27] The implication here is that only when the stations are owned and operated by the government might state action apply. But the fiduciary nature of the licensing system gives private station owners substantial latitude.

Finally, even in the clear case of government ownership of a broadcasting facility, the courts have rejected a finding of state action that could lead to application of a public forum model. In *Muir v. Alabama Education Television Commission* in 1982, the Fifth Circuit held that public television stations were not public forums.[28] Drawing on two previous Supreme Court decisions, the court held that there was no validity to the argument that simply "because a government facility is 'specifically used for the communication of information and ideas,' it is ipso facto a public forum."[29] In addition, the court found that public access would not be in keeping with the traditional usage of the facilities[30] and that the station itself maintained certain First Amendment protection for program content and control. The court stated:

The general invitation extended to the public is not to schedule programs, but to watch or decline to watch what is offered. It is thus clear that the public television stations involved in the cases before us are not public forums.[31]

A concurring opinion in the case did imply that in cable television, where some channels are offered for public access, strict content neutrality had to be observed,[32] but this has been noted in similar cases[33] and does not touch the situation in which the constitutional right to any cable access is in question.

While these cases are not completely determinative for cable, neither are they terribly encouraging. Had the decision in *CBS v. DNC* or even *Muir* gone the other way, a much stronger case for a public forum approach to cable's First Amendment status might have been built. Equally discouraging for this particular application is the holding in *Midwest Video II*, especially at the appellate level where access grounded in a First Amendment argument was rejected.[34]

Therefore, it appears that while a public forum model of cable rights might serve well the interests of the public and the cable operator, striking a balance between social and utilitarian supremacy, the requisite elements of public forum doctrine do not appear sufficiently in evidence in cable to provide for its application. Substantial problems in the area of state action and compatibility have been created by court decisions and the situation seems unlikely to change in the near future.

Notes

1. *See generally,* McLane, "Access to State Owned Communications Media The Public Forum Doctrine," 26 *U.C.L.A.L. Rev.* 1410 (1979).
2. 162 Mass. 510, 39 N.E. 113 (1895).
3. *See,* Kalven, "The Concept of the Public Forum: Cox v. Louisiana," 1965 *Sup. Ct. Rev.* 1 (1965) and Horning, "The First Amendment Right to a Public Forum," 1969 *Duke L. J.* 931 (1969).
4. 307 U.S. 496, 515 (1939).
5. *See,* Swartling, "The Public Forum Theory in Nontraditional Areas," 51 *Wash. L. Rev.* 143 (1975).
6. *See e.g., Grayned v. City of Rockford,* 408 U.S. 104 (1972) (restricting public areas immediately adjacent to public schools); *Garcia v. Gray,* 507 F.2d 539 (10th Cir. 1974) (restricting streets in residential areas); and *Concerned Jewish Youths v. McGuire,* 621 F.2d 471 (2d Cir. 1980) (suggesting special circumstances, such as a history of violent activity, may be sufficient to justify restrictions).
7. *Fernandes v. Limmer,* 663 F.2d 619 (5th Cir. 1981).
8. *Wolin v. Port of New York Authority,* 392 F.2d 83 (2nd Cir. 1968).
9. *Knights of Ku Klux Klan v. East Baton Rouge Parish School Board,* 578 F.2d 1122 (5th Cir. 1978), *on remand,* 643 F.2d 1034 (5th Cir. 1981).

10. *Dallas Ass'n of Community Organizations for Reform Now v. Dallas County Hospital District*, 670 F.2d 629 (5th Cir. 1982).

11. *Jeanette Rankin Brigade v. Chief of Capitol Police*, 342 F. Supp 575, aff'd, 409 U.S. 972 (1972).

12. *U.S. v. Grace*, 665 F.2d 1193 (D.C. Cir. 1981), *aff'd* 461 U.S. 171.

13. *See e.g., United States v. Abney*, 534 F.2d 984 (D.C. Cir. 1976).

14. *Police Department of Chicago v. Mosley*, 408 U.S. 92, 96 (1972).

15. *Marsh v. Alabama*, 326 U.S. 501 (1946).

16. *Food Employees v. Logan Valley Plaza*, 391 U.S. 308, 315 (1963).

17. *Grayned v. City of Rockford*, 408 U.S. 104 (1972).

18. *E.g., Gambino v. Fairfax County School Board*, 564 F.2d 157 (4th Cir. 1977) [although review of materials submitted to the publication under this doctrine may be reviewed by school authorities to insure factual accuracy; *see, Nicholson. v. Board of Education*, 682 F.2d 858 (9th Cir. 1982)].

19. *Southeastern Promotions Ltd. v. Conrad*, 420 U.S. 546 (1975).

20. 391 U.S. 308 (1968).

21. 407 U.S. 551 (1972).

22. 424 U.S. 507 (1976).

23. McLane, *supra.*

24. *Mississippi Gay Alliance v. Goudelock*, 536 F.2d 1073 (5th Cir. 1976).

25. *Muir v. Alabama Educational Television Commission*, 688 F.2d 1033 (5th Cir. 1982).

26. *Goudelock.*

27. *C.B.S. v. D.N.C.*, 412 U.S. 94, 116–121.

28. *Muir.*

29. *Muir* 688 F.2d at 1041, citing *U.S. Postal Service v. Council of Greenburgh Civic Associations*, 453 U.S. 114 (1981).

30. *Id.* at 1042.

31. *Id.*

32. *Id.* at 1050.

33. *E.g. City of Madison Joint School District v. Wisconsin Employment Commission*, 429 U.S. 167 (1976), and *Gay Activist Alliance v. Washington Metropolitan Area Transit Authority*, 5 Med. L. Rpt. 1404 (1979).

34. 571 F.2d 1025, 1055 (8th Cir. 1978).

9
The Public Utility Model

The Cable Communications Policy Act of 1984 specifically prohibits the regulation of cable TV as a common carrier or public utility. It remains, nonetheless, an important model to consider in forging a First Amendment framework for the medium, as the constitutional validity of the Cable Act is uncertain, and regulatory fashions change with political fancy. In any event, the consideration of cable television as a public utility is almost a tradition in regulatory debate. And, the positioning of cable television as a public utility is perhaps the oldest method of governmental oversight.

When states first began considering control of cable, the public utility model seemed an obvious choice, in part, because of the nebulous nature of public utilities as an industrial classification, and the ease with which government can declare a business to be invested with a public interest sufficient to justify economic intervention. The principal characteristics of a public utility are generally conceded to be the provision of an important public commodity or service and its position as a natural economic monopoly.[1] A precise definition of public utility and a general agreement on specific applications of the term have, however, historically escaped both regulators and judges. According to *Corpus Juris Secondim:*

> While the term has not been exactly defined, and . . . it would be difficult to construct a definition that would fit every conceivable case, the distinguishing characteristic of a public utility is the devotion of private property by the owner or person in control thereof to such a use that the public generally, or that part of the public which has been served and has accepted the service, has a right to demand that the use of the service, as long as it is continued, shall be conducted with reasonable efficiency and under proper charges.[2]

But whether or not a particular enterprise is impressed with an important public interest is quite necessarily dependent upon the facts of the particular case as perceived by the state.[3] The issue of the degree to which a given business is a natural economic monopoly is similarly wrapped in a hazy definitional shroud. Alfred Kahn, for example, asks rhetorically how "we cope with the historical fact that the prime historic exemplars of the extension of public utility regulation in the United States in the last quarter of the 19th century—railroads and grain elevators—were not really natural monopolists?"[4]

One long-settled controversy in public utility law is the validity of usurpation of private property for public purposes by the state in otherwise apparent contravention of the Fifth and Fourteenth Amendments. As early as 1876 the Supreme Court decided that certain industries were sufficiently "clothed" or "affected with the public interest" to overcome these constitutional barriers to state action.[5] The relatively strict boundaries the court drew around those industries specified as permissible public utilities[6] eventually gave way to a looser definitional position which recognized that nearly any modern business is vested with some public interest, and the only real constitutional barrier should be a procedural one to assure that the judgments of legislatures were not formed in a capricious or discriminatory manner.[7] It, therefore, has been left up to the legislatures, in the first instance, to determine whether a business is affected with a public interest and, so, subject to regulation.[8] But such determinations are subsequently subject to judicial review, and the decision as to what will be declared a public utility is ultimately one for the courts to make.[9]

Despite the vague standards and occasional lack of agreement on the application of public utility status, public utilities remain a fairly distinct group, comprising industries engaged in the generation and distribution of electrical power; the manufacture and distribution of gas; telephone and telegraph communications; common carrier transportation; local water supply and sewerage; and a variety of peripheral industries such as banking, irrigation and warehousing.[10] The application of the public utility model to cable raises several questions, including the definitional and constitutional validity of such an application and its philosophical utility.

Common Carriers

A special case of public utility regulation that is most closely associated with communications is that of the common carriers, most prominently telephone and telegraph. As noted in chapter 2, one of the early concerns in CATV regulation was the potential status of cable under Title II of the Communications Act, giving the commission regulatory power over common carriers.

Advocacy of a common carrier position for cable, either totally or in part, has been a recurrent theme in the debate over CATV control, and has persisted into modern legislative proposals.[11] It has been considered one approach to the equitable allocation of communication services to both individuals and to the community,[12] although usually with some fiat attached, such as waiting until the industry[13] or the individual cable company[14] grew to a sufficient, self-sustaining size. An early advocate of this approach was Ralph Lee Smith, who stated without equivocation that "Congress should . . . designate individual cable systems, and combined cable networks as common carriers, with access guaranteed to all comers."[15] More recently, Ithiel de Sola Pool has suggested government imposed access requirements as part of a full or partial common carrier approach to cable, predicting that public concern about the medium's monopoly status eventually will force such a role on cable.[16]

The consequences of a common carrier approach to cable TV are, as might be expected, radically different from those of a print or public forum model.

Application of the Model

As a common carrier, cable's service and the operation would fall under the jurisdiction of the FCC in a manner analogous to the telephone and telegraph. In addition, significant control over cable services would remain vested in state boards and commissions.[17] This control would extend into structure, behavior and content.

Structure. A common carrier model would presuppose no barriers to FCC regulation of ownership. Until recently, Congress has stipulated strict limits on foreign investment in domestic common carrier service,[18] and provided for FCC oversight of mergers and acquisitions in general.[19] In addition, there is nothing to suggest that restrictions applying to broadcast might not also apply to cable.

In a full common carrier model, access to the system would be provided on a nondiscriminatory, first-come, first-served basis; the cable operator would be permitted no discretion in the allocation of channels or services beyond that mandated by law.[20] Within the parameters of the guiding statutes, the operator would be stripped of editorial control over the system, and would act as a simple communications broker—a middleman between information supplier and information buyer.

In a partial common carrier model, such nondiscriminatory access would be proffered only on a certain number of channels—the number to be set by law[21]—with the cable operator maintaining greater or lesser control over the remaining channels in the system depending on whether they were governed under a public utility model or a print model.

Behavior. Permissible behavioral controls would be extensive. General technical oversight and authority over the management of the business would be common. Most construction, including the extension or termination of service to any given area, also would require federal and, perhaps, state approval.[22]

The issue of greatest importance to the cable operator might be rate regulation. The commission, in addition to the states, could be granted the power to oversee the establishment of rates for service, either for the entire system or for those channels allocated to common carrier service.[23] The determination of proper rates would be an important aspect of the promotion of free speech interests in that those unable to pay normal or prevailing rates would somehow have to be provided for. Ross argues that the stipulation of free or below-cost public access is out of keeping with a true common carrier model, which provides for a fair and equitable rate of return on capital investment.[24] But if considered in terms of cross-subsidization, the proposal for below-cost services seems neither unfair nor novel. Johnson notes, for example, that cost averaging, affording cross-subsidization among routes and services, historically has been a common guidepost in the regulation of telecommunication services.[25] And balancing rates to assure both a fair profit and minimal public service has been shown to be an attainable, if somewhat politically hazardous, task.

Content. In contrast to behavioral controls, controls on content would be severely circumscribed. The owner-operator would be prevented from exercising any "unjust or unreasonable discrimination in charges, practices, classifications, regulations, facilities or services,"[26] which arguably would include independent judgments as to the merit of the communication. At the same time, the owner-operator would be protected from liability for those transmissions beyond his or her authorized control. The state, too, in the form of the FCC or state regulatory commission, would be prevented from interfering in the cable communication by the strict standards of the First Amendment. Cable delivered expression would be protected, thereby, from censorship from both the government and the cable operator.

Critique

Commentators who have considered the FCC's role in common carrier regulation, in general, often begin by bemoaning (and then attempting to remedy) the lack of clear guidelines for ascertaining the status of a service as a common carrier.[27] Much of the confusion stems from the Communications Act's circularity with respect to the definition of common carrier. The act states that a common carrier means "any person engaged as a common carrier for hire."[28] The tautological language has forced most courts and critics to fall back on a plain language approach to the definition of a common carrier, which suggests a special service category of public utility engaged in the transport of goods and services, or in this case, the carriage of messages.[29]

As with the public forum approach, the first question, then, is one of definition. FCC staff skepticism about the applicability of common carrier regulations to cable was expressed as early as 1954,[30] and the formal opinion of the commission rejecting such an interpretation of common carrier rules was issued with a lengthy explanation in *Frontier Broadcasting v. Collier* in 1958.[31] The decision against regulating cable under Title II stemmed from the desired discretion of the cable operator to control routine programming. Cable exhibited several similarities to a common carrier, admitted the commission, but also demonstrated one important difference:

> This difference lies in the fact that the specific signals received and distributed by the CATV system are, of necessity, determined by the CATV system and not the subscriber. No individual subscriber has the option, nor may he compel the CATV system to receive and deliver a particular signal at a given time; nor has he the option or right to compel the station to receive and deliver signals different from or in addition to those offered and selected by the CATV system.[32]

This position was reaffirmed by the commission in its 1959 opinion declining cable control, and upheld by the D.C. Circuit Court of Appeals in 1966 in a case involving a Philadelphia television station which had requested that the FCC assert Title II authority over a local cable system.[33] Unfortunately, the court declined to address the substantive issue of whether a cable system was, in fact, a common carrier, deferring simply to the commission's prerogative to interpret its own enabling statute and finding the FCC choice in the matter both rational and permissible.

Subsequent to that case no substantial proposals beyond the musings of academics and part-time policy makers have come before the FCC or the courts in advocacy of a full common carrier status for cable.[34]

Proposals for a partial common carrier status for cable, generally in the form of mandated access channels, have been common, however. For example, the first invocation of access channel requirements by the FCC in 1972 did not meet with the pristine definition of common carrier status since the operator was obliged in numerous ways to oversee access to, and the content of, the channels. As a result, the American Civil Liberties Union (ACLU) filed a lawsuit in 1975 arguing against operator oversight of access and in favor of a strict common carrier approach to the use of those channels.[35] The Ninth Circuit, with some candor, noted that the ACLU position was not without some merit,[36] but echoing the D.C. Circuit in the Philadelphia TV case, the judge deferred to commission authority and found, according to *Southwestern,* that the rules were "reasonably ancillary."[37]

Subsequently, of course, the Supreme Court, in *Midwest Video II* (1979), ruled that even this modest level of enforced access represented the imposition of common carrier-like regulations, and that such control was beyond the jurisdiction of the FCC. The broadcast model the High Court applied did not permit such interference.

Although the court's holding does not attack the question directly here— the issue being the constitutional permissibility and wisdom of a common carrier model, not the statutory authority of the commission to impose one— in connection with the other decisions noted, it suggests the general difficulty in applying such a model. At the outset, cable may not meet the definitional criteria of a common carrier, for it does not seek of its own volition to provide such a service, either totally or in part. Even to the extent that public and leased access channels may be tendered, authority to delimit the nature of use and user is often sought by the company. Finally, even if one were to concede the definitional argument, the question of the philosophical and practical utility remains.

If one returns, then, to the assumption of the predominance of the individually oriented model of First Amendment rights, the inescapable question for the common carrier model, as for all the collectivistically oriented models, is the existence and nature of the special circumstances that would permit state interference on behalf of the public. Examination of this important question is reserved for later discussion for two reasons. First, the consideration is equally applicable to the broader public utility model and will be dealt with in the next section; and second, there are sufficient philosophical problems with the common carrier model that the special circumstances question need not be raised at this time.

Plainly put, an application of a full common carrier model of First Amendment rights would not strike the desired balance between collectivistic and individualistic expressive goals. As the print model provides no latitude for the servicing of community goals (beyond those that accrue naturally), the common carrier model provides no latitude for the servicing of potential First Amendment interests of the cable operator. This model represents the far end of the social supremacy category, stripping the owner of the means of communication of nearly all editorial discretion. It is quite analogous to proposals requiring newspapers to turn their facilities of publication and distribution over to all on a first-come, first-served basis,[38] proposals that run far afield of traditional First Amendment interpretation. While it is quite possible that the common carrier model would effectively serve the needs of the society for an open flow of dialogue, it offends the interests of the individual owner-operator and fails to provide for a proper compromise between the two. In short, a full common carrier model is flawed in a variety of important dimensions and must be rejected.

Public Utility

A partial common carrier, one that calls for the provision of a limited, specified number of access channels, may not suffer from the same weaknesses, but neither is it a true common carrier. At the same time, as common carriers are only a special case of the broader universe of public utilities, cable does not have to be labeled as a common carrier for the range of public utility regulation to apply. The states historically have regulated cable television as a public utility without designating it as a common carrier. Some states have declared, through administrative or legislative action, that cable television is a public utility subject to the attendant substantive and procedural public utility guidelines.[39] Other states have simply invested within their public utilities commissions or departments the power to oversee the operation of cable without specifically declaring it a public utility.[40] In those states that have not established a general state-wide regulatory policy toward cable, proposals for such regulation have historically taken the form of a public utility model.

Legislative proposals to declare CATV a public utility began appearing almost as soon as cable did. Pennsylvania considered regulating cable television as a public utility as early as 1955, Arizona, Montana, and Washington as early as 1957.[41] And such proposals continue to be offered today. Illinois is a modern example. S.B. 1484, introduced in the 1982 state legislature, would include cable in the state's definition of a public utility.[42]

Even the federal government has considered the relationship between CATV and public utilities generally in the course of debate over the appropriate roles of federal and state oversight of the medium. In 1966, for example, the FCC argued that, for many important purposes, cable television could and should be considered a public utility subject to state regulation. Commission Chairman E. William Henry told the House Interstate Commerce Commission, meeting that year on proposed cable legislation, that while cable could not be considered a common carrier it did have many attributes of a public utility; the states, therefore, should retain authority over such matters as rate regulation, extension of service, and choice of entry.[43] This position was attacked vigorously in the hearings by representatives of the cable industry. The National Cable Television Association submitted a detailed rebuttal entitled "A CATV System is Not of a Public Utility Nature," in which it argued against the public utility and common carrier rationales for state, local, and federal regulation of service and rate.[44]

Moreover, the early failure of federal legislation in cable, including the death of the bills under consideration in 1966, coupled with the FCC's increasing unwillingness to involve itself with cable had, until recently, left the states relatively free to continue their growing efforts at cable regulation, efforts that often took public utility form.

The wave of federal cable deregulation bills in the early 1980s and the final passage of the Cable Communications Act altered that state of affairs somewhat by limiting state and local power. The effect has been to spur several states to abandon regulation, disband their cable boards and transfer oversight to more general governing bodies.[45] At the same time, regulation that is in substance, if not in name, born of a public utilities model continues in other states.

Application of the Model: Structure, Behavior, and Content

Control under a public utility model necessarily favors the collective, providing a very different set of operating rules than does the print model; no substantial barriers exist to requirements governing a multitude of structural and behavioral aspects. For example, industry structure within a state could be closely monitored and manipulated. Franchise terms specifying the length of the contract, its geographic area, and certain qualifying characteristics of potential operators are illustrative of permissible rules and characteristic of many state and local regulations. While much less typical in practice, cross-ownership restrictions limiting the interest a cable operator may hold in other media in the area are also arguably permissible controls under the public utility model. Access, of course, would be a major component of any public utility scheme for cable, and is a standard requirement of most states which assert such authority.

Similarly, a public utility model would permit a broad range of behavioral controls over the cable operator. To meet the public interest standard, the operator would have to seek approval for, and justify any extension or changes in, service and any increase or modification in rates. In addition, the government could impose service requirements such as the provision by the company of equipment and studios for public access programming, and perhaps even ascertainment by the operator of local community needs. All these requirements could easily be accommodated by a model of First Amendment rights that placed primary value on the interests of the community.

Less clear is the balance that would have to be struck between the operator and the community regarding content. Until recently, few guidelines existed in this matter outside the common carrier regulations which stripped the owner-operator of all editorial discretion. The broader public utility model is less restrictive of owner rights and implies some functioning of the operator as an independent message provider. Traditional constraints on this role have, however, included restrictions similar to Fairness Doctrine and Equal Time as well as regulations governing commercial and obscene and indecent speech. A straightforward approach to regulation as a public utility, then, might suggest little operator recourse in the event of state or local demands or restraints on programming practices. On the other hand, a 1980 Supreme Court decision involving the First Amendment rights of public utilities may serve to soften this older view and supply cable owners with rights not previously suspected under the public utility model. In *Consolidated Edison Co. of New York v. Public Service Commission of New York*,[46] the court said that public utilities do have some degree of First Amendment protection for the expression of their controversial views. The issue sprang from 1976 Consolidated Edison billing insert on nuclear energy. A citizens group sought to have a rebuttal message included in future Con Ed billings, but the Public Service Commission (PSC) declined their request. In addition, the PSC forbade the company from issuing similar inserts of its own. The company appealed the ruling on First Amendment grounds.

In dissent, Justice Harry Blackmun, with Justice Rehnquist, argued that the extensive state power over public utilities included the authority to regulate expressive activities in the interest of the public, and that other forums existed for the company's speech.[47] This represented, perhaps, a classical extension of the authority given the state to regulate structural and behavioral aspects of the public utility sector. The seven-member majority disagreed, however. Justice Powell, writing for the court, found that Con Ed was entitled, as a corporation, to substantial First Amendment rights:

> Nor does Consolidated Edison's status as a privately owned but government regulated monopoly preclude its assertion of First Amendment rights. We have recognized that the speech of a heavily regulated business may enjoy constitutional protection. Consolidated Edison's position as a regulated monopoly does not decrease the information value of its opinions on critical public matters.[48]

How far that protection might extend is left ambiguous by the decision. While some protection is proffered in the case, the facts may not be analogous to cable given the medium of expression about which the court concerns itself. Much is made in the decision of the difference between broadcasting and its permissible level of regulation and the medium at hand—the postal service. The court noted that scarcity, which might justify such regulation, does not exist in this case, and that the presence of the bill inserts in question would not preclude other inserts which the PSC might lawfully order.[49] The decision implies First Amendment protection for the speech of a public utility, but that protection may be limited to the facts of the case, specifically use of the mails, and so it is difficult to draw any but the most tenuous parallels to cable.

Eventual extension of the *Con Ed* decision to cable might move the public utility model closer to that of the broadcasting model, in that both would permit a significant degree of government control over structure and behavior but limit control over content. Absent such an extension, however, the public utility model must be considered as more liberal than the broadcast approach in the degree of power it grants to government in all areas, including content. It suggests a regulatory scheme short of the common carrier model which leaves the owner-operator without any editorial discretion, but less considerate of owner rights than the broadcast model.

Critique

Philosophical Considerations. As the above discussion suggests, the public utility model of cable First Amendment rights would fall on the social utility continuum somewhere between the social goals and social supremacy archetypes. It casts information and communication as important social needs—services provided for the general welfare—and grants state oversight on the basis of an economic monopoly of that service. There are concessions to the First Amendment rights of the system operator, the individual, making the model less severe with respect to those rights than the common carrier approach. Unlike that model, a public utilities scenario seeks to assure that access to the communication system is provided for all members of the community while at the same time attempting to protect the right of the operator to use the system for communicative purposes as well. There is, then, some attempt at balance here.

Nonetheless, there are within the model multiple avenues for suppression of individual (cablecaster) speech even though they may be innocent in intent. While *Consolidated Edison* provides a degree of protection for the First Amendment rights of public utilities using the mails, it may not extend to a situation in which the system of communication itself is the utility. Further, the framework of regulatory constraints on structure and behavior that accompanies a public utility model may be just as effective as direct suppression of speech in acting as prior restraints. Ownership restrictions, access regulations, and service requirements that indirectly mandate or prohibit certain programming practices (e.g., obligatory community access centers) may all contribute to restrict the range of editorial discretion permitted the system operator. The model appears, therefore, to balance too heavily on the side of the collective. At the very least, its ability to fully service the First Amendment rights of the cablecaster are suspect. On philosophical grounds alone, then, it is a weak candidate for an equitable protection model.

Practical Considerations. There are two problems that must be addressed in considering the legitimate practical application of the public utility model to cable. First, does the definition fit? Is cable a public utility within the legal and historic sense of the word? If it is not, then there are no grounds, at the outset, for a consideration of special circumstances that would overwhelm the assumed First Amendment preference of individual protection. Second, if it can be successfully argued that cable does meet the proper criteria, is cable's standing as a public utility sufficient cause to overcome the First Amendment interests of the individual, that is, is there a sufficient special circumstance to trigger the search for a balancing of individual and collective rights?

A review of decision making here, at the legislative, administrative, and judicial levels, provides guidance only to the extent of outlining and specifying the issues. Proposals for solutions are rare, and agreement on those proposals rarer still. As noted, state legislatures and administrative agencies have often concluded that cable is a public utility, but numerous other states—sometimes with the same amount of consideration, and sometimes without it—have concluded just the opposite. In the early years of cable, the attorneys general of both Arizona[50] and New Mexico[51] determined that cable was not a public utility. The Public Utility Commission (PUC) of Utah ruled the same in 1958.[52] But, as with the regulating states, there is little indication that the determination wasn't more political than rational.

A forum providing a better record of consideration is the court system. The issues appear more clearly defined in the court cases and, again, the courts have been given final jurisdiction in determining the legitimacy of state action establishing public utilities. Two early cases illustrating the conflict and ambiguity are *Greater Freemont v. City of Freemont*[53] and *TV Pix, Inc. v. Taylor*[54] in 1968.

In *TV Pix*, a federal district court in Nevada concluded that the use of public streets, alleys, byways, and other property over which the cable company needed to lay wire, plus the probable designation of cable as a natural monopoly, supported designation of CATV as a public utility:

> As the facts appear from the record before us and the controlling precedents, there is no reason to conclude that community antenna service is not monopolistic in character and is not affected with the public interest. State supervision of it as a public utility does not conflict with the Fourteenth Amendment.[55]

But in *Greater Freemont*, the issue of cable's classification as a public utility also was considered, with the court in that case coming to just the opposite conclusion. In addition to noting that cable had similarities to other protected media, the court found that cable lacked requisite elements that delineated a public utility, those being significant public need and a position as a monopolistic or oligopolistic industry. Explained the judge:

> The first of these characteristics clearly is not present. The public has about as much real need for the service of a CATV system as it does for hand

carved ivory back-scratchers. Even if in fact the CATV system is the only one in the market, it is not a monopoly in the economic sense.[56]

The court based its latter comment on a finding that there was no great public inconvenience in the stringing of additional wires by competing companies, and until recently, the question of economic scarcity has not been pursued by the courts. Instead, attention has focused on the question of the public's need for cable television. Is cable a service so necessary to the public welfare that it classifies as a public utility?

In the House Interstate Commerce Committee hearings in 1966, FCC Chairman Henry argued that cable did provide a necessary public service, citing as support the amount of mail received by the commission whenever "the public thought that its television service might be lost."[57] Although the reasoning has been somewhat more substantive, many state courts have agreed.[58] The New York Supreme Court, for example, has twice ruled that cable is adequately invested with sufficient public interest to support a finding of public utility status.[59] According to the court, cable "provides basically the same public service as non-cable television and is so imbued with a public interest that it classifies as a public utility."[60]

Few courts, however, have specified the nature of the essential public service provided by cable, save for commenting on the general need for telecommunication services. Is this a need equivalent to that for water and power? What fundamental human requirements are serviced here? In *White v. City of Ann Arbor,* the Michigan Supreme Court attempted an answer, ruling, as had the court in *TV Pix,* that cable was indeed a similar service to the provision of water, gas, power, and sewage treatment.[61] And, in concurrence, Judge Moody explained that it was the cultural and psychological needs of society that cable served:

> While cable television may not cater to the physical needs of man as do utilities that provide heat, light and power, it provides an equally important service in terms of the rational, psychological and aesthetic growth process of man. Further, as many commentators adroitly point out, cable television is in its essence a de facto monopoly.[62]

In contrast, the position of the National Cable TV Association has been that cable is not an essential service. The public good accruing from cable television can be equally derived from other entertainment and information sources, according to the industry. Cable, therefore, is at best a luxury service. Noted NCTA officials during the 1966 Congressional hearings:

> CATV systems make available to their subscribers either a greater choice of television signals than they would have without CATV service or improved quality of the pictures viewed on their television sets. In a sense this

is a luxury service and luxury services have not been made subject to public utility regulation in the past.[63]

In striking down asserted PUC jurisdiction in the states, some courts have avoided the definitional problem, basing their decisions on the narrow language of state law. California courts, for example, have repeatedly declared that cable is not a public utility within the meaning of that term as set down by the language of the state constitution.[64] But where the issue has been specifically joined, the courts have not been hesitant to side with the NCTA, as illustrated by the decision in *Greater Freemont* in the observation that the public need for cable television was about as severe as the public need for "hand carved ivory back scratchers."

More recently, the Washington State Supreme Court ruled that cable was not a necessary service. Dicta in *City of Issaquah v. Teleprompter* in 1980 points to a view of cable not at all in keeping with Judge Moody's assessment.[65] Cable is essentially "a luxury service," said the court, "a television improvement."[66] The value of cable television as it relates to public utility status remains, it seems, most problematic.

A related, and equally unresolved, question—addressed earlier in a different context—is the legitimacy of regulation as a public utility in conjunction with cable's use of public thoroughfares. Scholars such as de Sola Pool support the legitimacy of such a rationale,[67] and some courts have agreed. In *City of Owensboro v. Top Vision Cable Co. of Kentucky*, the court ruled that cable television was, in fact, a public utility and, as such, the local franchise ordinance was a legitimate exercise of power based on the city's right to control streets, alleys, and public grounds.[68]

In contrast, the Kansas Supreme Court, in the first of two related decisions, ruled cable to be a private business and numerous local franchise requirements based on the police power over use of public thoroughfares to be invalid.[69] The court declared that regulations based on that police power must have some reasonable relationship to the use of streets and alleys. The franchise in question restricted a variety of business and programming activities of the cable company, including hours during which the business office had to be open and provision of local access channels. Said the court:

> We do not believe that the requirements and provisions in the ordinance heretofore summarized have any rational relationship to the use and rightful regulation of the city streets. They deal more with the management of the internal affairs of a CATV system which for our review here must be considered as a commercial enterprise.[70]

The court's decision was subsequently overturned by the state legislature, which expressly gave the city the right to franchise on the basis of its power over public streets. The law provided the following:

The furnishing of cable television service by means of facilities in place in the public ways, streets and alleys is hereby declared to be a private business affected with such public interest by reason of its use of public ways, alleys and streets so as to require that it be reasonably regulated by the cities.[71]

The court, in *Capitol Cable, Inc. v. City of Topeka,* conceded the debate to the legislature by concluding that the status of cable television—public utility or private enterprise—was a question of law, not a question of fact, and was settled, therefore, by the state's action.[72]

If the conclusion of the Kansas court is valid, and the mercurial definition of public utility suggests it may be, then there is little outside federal law to deter the states from holding that cable television is, indeed, a public utility, arguments to the contrary notwithstanding. It seems to come down to a rather subjective evaluation as to the social value of cable television. It is very shaky ground upon which to base constitutional law. It is perhaps best to concede, at least arguendo, that cable could be declared a public utility, thereby raising the subsequent question of whether that designation is a sufficient special circumstance to overcome the First Amendment rights of the operator.

In fact, the three elements that coalesce to form the grounds for public utility status already have been examined in one form or another in this study and found wanting. The issue of cable's position as an economic monopoly has been considered at length and, due to the holding in *Tornillo,* rejected as a basis for state control. The proposition that the use of public thoroughfares is adequate justification for an affirmative reading of the First Amendment has also been considered and rejected as in *Preferred.* An argument that the public interest inherent in cable television service is sufficient justification for government control is, in its broadest philosophical sense, simply a restatement of the notion that the rights of the collective should carry greater weight than the rights of the individual in First Amendment law. This, then, becomes circular logic, rather than an exposition of special circumstances that would justify a reversal of established doctrine.

More broadly, the *Consolidated Edison* case demonstrates that the state may not inhibit the First Amendment rights of a public utility, but it does not address a situation in which the function of the asserted utility is inextricably bound up in the business of communication and expression. The medium that most strongly parallels cable in this context may again be the newspaper industry. It already has been demonstrated that newspapers are, as cable, vested with such economies of scale that monopoly situations have become the norm. At the same time, the public service provided by a newspaper is without question; it is, quite probably, much easier to argue the public need for a newspaper than for cable television. In fact, the nature of a newspaper as a public service has been commented upon by the courts. In

United States v. Harte-Hanks Newspapers, a U.S. district court held that a newspaper company that purchased a competitor was not in violation of antitrust laws because a newspaper held a position as a "quasi-public service."[73] The Supreme Court, in *Tornillo,* noted such arguments, stating:

> It is urged that the claim of newspapers to be "surrogates of the public" carries with it a concomitant fiduciary obligation to account for that stewardship. From this premise it is reasoned that the only effective way to insure fairness and accuracy and to provide for some accountability is for government to take affirmative action.[74]

But the court rejected the validity of such claims. In general, the courts have not recognized economic scarcity, public interest, or public utility status alone as grounds for assertion of affirmative action.

Conclusions

It can be argued that cable television meets the definitional requirements of a public utility. At least, it seems possible that legislative bodies could, with some impunity, declare them as such. The public utility model fails, nonetheless, to provide the kind of mechanism sought to balance the interests of the individual and the society in a cable context.

Philosophically, the model tends to overbalance in favor of the collective; it leaves a great deal of room, perhaps too much room, for governmental control that could result in de facto prior restraints.

Practically, the model fails to provide the special circumstances apparently necessary for the courts to justify government intervention in the First Amendment rights of the individual. To the extent that states have regulated cable companies as public utilities, then, they would seem to have done so in direct violation of the First Amendment, especially when such regulation entailed the direct or indirect control of practices that affect programming or programming decisions.

While superficially attractive as a possible mechanism for achieving a balance in First Amendment rights, the public utility model, like the public forum model, falls short. Realizing the goal of making cable a First Amendment forum for both owner and consumer may, therefore, require a new way of thinking about the application of constitutional law to the media in general. That is the topic of the final chapter.

Notes

1. *See generally,* 73B C.J.S. *Public Utilities* secs. 1, 2, 14.
2. 73B C.J.S. *Public Utilities* sec. 2.

3. 73B C.J.S. *Public Utilities* sec. 3.

4. A. Kahn, *The Economics of Regulation: Principles and Institutions,* vol. 1 at 12 (NY: John Wiley & Sons, Inc., 1970).

5. *Munn v. Illinois,* 94 U.S. 113 (1876).

6. *E.g., Munn,* (grain elevators); *Noble State Bank v. Haskell,* 219 U.S. 104 (1911) (banks); *German Alliance Insurance Co. v. Lewis,* 233 U.S. 389 (1914) (fire insurance companies); and *O'Gorman & Young, Inc. v. Hartford Fire Insurance Co.,* 282 U.S. 251 (1931) (insurance agents).

7. *Nebbia v. New York,* 291 U.S. 502, at 536–37 (1934).

8. *See, Gulf States Utilities Co. v. State,* 46 S.W.2d 1018 (1938).

9. *See,* 73B C.J.S. *Public Utilities* sec. 2.

10. Kahn, *supra,* at 10.

11. *See, e.g.,* S. 2172, 97th Cong. 1st Sess. (1982).

12. *See, e.g.,* I. de Sola Pool, *Technologies of Freedom,* 239–40 (Cambridge, MA: Belknap Press, 1983); B. Owen, *Communications for Tomorrow: Policy Perspectives for the 1980s,* 240–42, (New York: Praeger Publishers, 1978) (advocating a common carrier scheme as the least intrusive means of controlling the new technology); *The Sloan Commission: On The Cable,* 46–48 (New York: McGraw Hill, 1971) (suggesting that eventual consideration of cable as a common carrier might be desirable); W. Jones, "Regulation of Television by the State of New York, Report to the State of New York Public Service Commission," 199 (1970).

13. *Id.,* Sloan.

14. *Id.,* Jones.

15. R. Smith, *The Wired Nation,* 90 (New York: Harper and Row, 1972).

16. *Id.,* de Sola Pool at 173.

17. *See, e.g.,* 47 U.S.C. sec. 221(b) (1962) (relating to state authority over common carriers).

18. 47 U.S.C. sec. 222(d) (1962).

19. 47 U.S.C. sec. 222(b) (1962).

20. 47 U.S.C. sec. 201(a),(1962).

21. *See, e.g.,* S. 2172.

22. *E.g.,* 47 U.S.C. sec. 214(a) (1962).

23. *E.g.,* 47 U.S.C. sec. 205(a) (1962).

24. L. Ross, *Economic and Legal Foundations of Cable Television,* 54 (Beverly Hills: Sage Publications, 1974).

25. L. Johnson, "Boundaries to Monopoly and Regulation in Telecommunications," in *Communications for Tomorrow,* 127–28.

26. 47 U.S.C. sec. 202(a) (1962).

27. *See e.g.,* M. Hall, "Common Carriers Under the Communications Act," 48 *U. Chi. L. Rev.* 409 (1981), or K. O'Riordan, "An Examination of the Application of Common Carrier Regulation to Entities Providing New Telecommunications Services, 29 *Case W. Res.* 577 (1979).

28. 47 U.S.C. sec. 153(h) (1982).

29. Much of the language of the Communications Act is, of course, drawn from earlier laws concerning the regulation of common carriers such as railroads, *see,* H.

Friendly, *The Federal Administrative Agencies,* 54–55 (Cambridge, MA: Harvard University Press, 1962).

30. Memorandum Opinion and Order in Belnap and Associates, 18 F.C.C. 642 (1954).

31. 24 F.C.C. 251 (1958).

32. *Id.* at 254.

33. *Philadelphia Television Boradcasting v. F.C.C.,* 359 F.2d 282 (D.C. Cir. 1966).

34. *See e.g.,* M. Nadel, "COMCAR: A Marketplace Cable Television Franchise Structure," 20 *Harv. J. on Legis.* 541 (1983).

35. 523 F.2d 1344 (9th Cir. 1975).

36. *Id.* at 1350.

37. *Id.* at 1351.

38. B. Owen, *Economics and Freedom of Expression,* 58 (Cambridge, MA: Ballinger Publishing Co., 1975).

39. *E.g.,* Conn. Gen. Stat. ch. 227, sec. 16; Delaware, Del. Code Ann., title 26; Alaska, Alaska Stat. sec. 42.05.701(8); Nevada, Nev. Rev. Stat. sec. 711.020.

40. *E.g.,* New Jersey, N.J. Stat. Ann., 48:5A; Vermont, Vt. Stat. Ann., tit. 30, sec. 501; and Hawaii, Hawaii Rev. Stat. sec. 440-G.

41. *E.g.,* Pennsylvania, H.B. 835 (1955); West Virginia, H.B. 397 (1955); Arizona, H.C.R. 12 (1957); Montana, S.B. 184 (1957); Washington, S.B. 425 (1957); Oregon, H.B. 1564 (1961); and Arkansas, H.B. 309 (1963).

42. It was, however, the tenth year in a row that such a bill had been introduced in the Illinois state house without passage. *See, Interaction,* newsletter of the National Cable Television Association, May 1982, at 12.

43. *Regulation of Community Antenna Television: Hearings on H.R. 12914, H.R. 13286, and H.R. 14201 Before the House Comm. on Interstate and Foreign Commerce,* 89th Cong., 1st Sess. 49–51 (1966).

44. *Id.* at 489–520.

45. *See e.g.,* Nev. A. 505 (1985) and Minn. H. 786 (1985).

46. 447 U.S. 530 (1980).

47. *Id.* at 549.

48. *Id.* at 533–34.

49. *Id.* at 543.

50. 12 R.R. 2094 (1955).

51. 10 R.R. 2058 (1954).

52. 14 R.R. 2063 (1956).

53. 302 F. Supp. 652 (N.D. Ohio 1968).

54. 304 F. Supp. 459 (D. Nev. 1968).

55. *Id.* at 467.

56. 302 F. Supp. at 665.

57. *Regulation of Community Antenna Television, supra* note 43, at 50.

58. *White v. City of Ann Arbor,* 281 N.W.2d 283 (1979); *White v. Detroit Edison,* 263 N.W.2d 367 (1978); *Crowley v. New York Telephone Co.,* 363 N.Y.S.2d 292 (1975); *Staminski v. Romeo,* 310 N.Y.S.2d 169 (1970); *Aberdeen Cable TV Service v. Aberdeen,* 176 N.W.2d 738 (1970); *In re Cokeville Radio and Electric*

Co., 6 P.U.R.3d 129 (1954); *Independent Theater Owners of Arkansas v. Arkansas PSC*, 361 S.W.2d 642 (1962), (although at least one court has upheld PSC jurisdiction without a finding that cable was a public utility, *In re Cable TV*, 332 A.2d 209 (1974).

59. *Staminski*, 310 N.Y.S.2d 169, and *Hoffman v. Capitol Cablevision Systems, Inc.*, 372 N.Y.S.2d 482 (1975).

60. *Hoffman*, 372 N.Y.S.2d at 484.

61. 281 N.W.2d at 289.

62. *Id.* at 290 (Moody, J. concurring).

63. *Regulation of Community Antenna Television supra* note 43, at 499.

64. *Television Transmission, Inc. v. P.U.C.*, 301 P.2d 862 (1956), and *Orange County Cable Communications Co. v. City of San Clemente*, 59 C.A.3d 165 (1976).

65. 611 P.2d 741 (1980).

66. *Id.* at 745.

67. *Supra*, de Sola Pool at 240.

68. 487 S.W.2d 283 (1972).

69. *Community Antenna Television of Wichita, Inc. v. City of Wichita*, 471 P.2d 360 (1970).

70. *Id.* at 365.

71. *See Capital Cable, Inc. v. City of Topeka*, D. Kan. 495 P.2d 885, 891 (1972).

72. *Id.* at 892.

73. 170 F. Supp. 227, 228 (1959).

74. 418 U.S. 241, 251 (1974).

10
The Equitable Protection Model

Thus far, the analysis points to two related conclusions: first, under current, proper constitutional interpretation, most of the controls now applied to cable television are violations of the First Amendment rights of cable owners and operators; and second, a model for providing for the First Amendment interests of the collective must, therefore, entail some reinterpretation or modification of constitutional law.

To elaborate on the first point: It has been argued that the presumption of First Amendment protection rests classically with the individual in situations in which there is an apparent conflict with the First Amendment interests of the collective. Further, in order to initiate controls that would strike a balance between the two, some special circumstances must be shown to exist. Scarcity of channels in broadcasting is the prime example.

The problem in cable is an apparent lack of special circumstances that would justify state intervention on the behalf of the collective. A scarcity argument akin to that put forth in broadcasting fails. The multiplicity of channels available via cablecasting is the medium's primary attribute, and there is little support for a contention that technical barriers exist to the establishment of multiple, competing cable systems. The barrier to competitive situations is economic, not technical, but the Supreme Court apparently has refused to accept the argument that economic scarcity is adequate reason for government intervention in First Amendment rights.

A holding that cable is a necessary social service might lead to the development of a public utility position, but it is an arguable notion and, even if accepted, leaves too much room for possible state interference with cable-caster rights. Regulation based on the use of streets and alleys, it has been suggested, is reasonable grounds for regulating the laying and maintenance of wire, but little beyond that—certainly not the control of content or access by the state. The ancillarity doctrine merely describes the outer limits of permissible government control; it does not act as a special circumstance for the assertion of such control. The application of the interstate communication clause of the Communication Act, which does act as such a lever, might not pass a test of its constitutionality. Any of these paths to control might serve as a vehicle for state action and, hence, lead to a public forum approach, but without them, that model cannot be legitimately called upon.

The most appropriate model of First Amendment rights for cable television under existing law seems, therefore, to be the print model. Under this model, however, nearly all the federal, state, and local controls currently imposed upon cable television are unconstitutional violations of the First Amendment. It would be unthinkable for government at any level to attempt to license books or magazines. Regulations that restrict ownership or market entry in the print media have been soundly rejected by the courts, as have attempts to institute state-compelled access to newspapers. Beyond the regulation of normal business activity that even newspapers are subject to, government control of cable television would seem in violation of the First Amendment. This, in turn, means that the system of local franchising is unconstitutional. General state oversight by cable boards or public utilities commissions, likewise, ought to be struck down under existing law, and the same holds for federal regulation. There are simply no easily defensible justifications for such constraints. They act as prior restraints on speech and, without a new approach to the First Amendment, must ultimately be rescinded.

But while acceptance of the print model and rejection of general state control appears the logical answer, it does not satisfy the philosophical aims outlined earlier. The quest here is for an approach to cable television that provides for social as well as individual First Amendment interests. The print model clearly does not do this. The reality of the industry is such that monopoly situations do appear inevitable in cable television, making one person or company the gatekeeper for all information about, and opinion over, cable in a given area.

A possible solution that would not entail a change in law or constitutional interpretation would be the ownership of cable television systems by the state. While municipal ownership is not typical, neither is it unheard of. Some cable systems are owned by the cities in which they operate. Cities may write into their original franchise agreements with private companies the right to buy the system at a later date, and some have exercised that option.[1] Other cities may seek to build their own system at the outset, establishing an independent board to oversee the operation.[2]

There are numerous advantages to such a system. The state would not infringe on the First Amendment rights of individuals by way of cable controls since private owner-operators would not be involved. State ownership is perhaps the purest form of state action and, despite *Muir,* might open a public forum for the expression of the full spectrum of community views. The state, therefore, could not deny access to those seeking it. Any attempt to prevent such expression would be prohibited by the constitutional protection against prior restraint by the state. Time, place, amd manner controls in the form of nondiscriminatory regulations governing the scheduling of such programming (time and channel slots) would be the only permissible limitations on public expression over the system.[3]

The problem with this proposal is that it represents more of a circumvention of the problem than a solution to it. It does not seek a balance of collective and individual rights; it simply avoids the problem by doing away with the demands (in this context) of the individual First Amendment aims. It prevents a confrontation between the two rather than resolving the confrontation. More practically, it ignores the fact that the vast majority of cable systems are privately owned and are very likely to stay that way for a long time. While a city may buy a cable system currently under private ownership, it may not normally, in keeping with either the First or the Fifth Amendments, simply seize the system in the name of the state and for the good of the expressive interests of society. Finally, despite assurances that the First Amendment really is a strong protection against state tampering or illegitimate control of the system, many still hold a deep fear of a state run communications system. For many, the specter of propaganda and political manipulation resides within such proposals. A state owned cable system, then, does not appear to be the practical alternative.

The Failed Market Theory Reconsidered

It is useful to reconsider the failed market theory here because it lies at the heart of the problem itself, that problem being the potential domination of a system of communications by one company, individual, or government. The threat of monopoly or oligopoly positioning in cable communications leads to the difficult consideration of the often opposing interests of individual and collective. It is, after all, market forces that tend to constrict the libertarian ideal and frustrate the operation of a system of freedom of expression that would benefit both. Were freedom of entry into the market a reality, there would be little chance of a confrontation between individual and social rights, for the variety of ideas and views necessary for a healthy polity would find no strong barriers to distribution.

It is this concern about monopoly control, of course, that has led Congress to require equal access to broadcast facilities for political candidates, and the government to attempt to impose community access requirements on cable. It is also the motivating force behind access proposals for newspapers, such as those advocated by Barron and others. The stumbling block, as has been noted here repeatedly, is the Supreme Court's refusal to acknowledge this situation as a legitimate foundation for the construction of an affirmative interpretation of the First Amendment for newspapers. In

Tornillo, the court candidly admitted the severity of the situation and even seemed sympathetic to access proponents, but it declined to give those concerns sufficient weight to overcome the traditionally powerful barriers to government intervention in newspaper publishing. This decision, as much as any other, has frustrated advocates of an affirmative reading of the First Amendment and prevented rational adoption of several already reviewed models of cable First Amendment rights.

The suggestion advanced here, and the key to an equitable protection theory of cable rights, is that *Tornillo* has been interpreted too broadly, or, at the very least, could be reinterpreted to permit the fashioning of First Amendment theory based on a failed market perspective without disturbing the narrower holding as it applied to the specific facts of the case. A different approach to *Tornillo* and the general question of access to the various media systems could offer the means for a fair balancing of social and individual interests in cable TV.

The first step is a stricter delineation of the distinguishing characteristics of different media. As noted in the first chapter, some theorists have called for a First Amendment framework that extends equal protection and responsibilities to all media, creating a unified field theory of First Amendment rights. The court, however, has shown no sign of accepting such proposals and maintains an apparent position of establishing different sets of rules for different media. Each medium, then, must be judged separately in its ability to serve the interests of the individual and the collective.

The various media systems can be divided for these purposes along several dimensions, including industry economics, message production, and social impact.[4] But classically, media definitions have centered around the methods of message maintenance and distribution. How the message is transmitted and how it is kept viable during that transmission are the related parameters that have seemed most pertinent to the court.[5] Accordingly, media break down in the general categories of speech, cinema, print, broadcasting, and cable. Each has a common sense definition, but specification along the lines outlined above may help prevent ambiguity. Specifically, speech is limited in distribution to those within earshot of the speaker and in duration by the ability of the sound wave to maintain the message. Cinema is maintained by the mechanism of film and is distinguished from television movies by a distribution system that relies on public theaters. Print is a system of symbols (as distinguished from cinema) imposed on a relatively permanent vehicle such as paper and distributed physically by a messenger system of greater or lesser sophistication.[6]

Broadcasting is chiefly characterized by the use of the electromagnetic spectrum for over-the-air distribution of programming. Cable varies from broadcasting, of course, in the use of physical cable, either coaxial or fiberoptical, to move the electronic impulses that form the message. The media can, thereby, be distinguished technically, and such differences may serve as the foundation for First Amendment distinctions.

The important second step in the process is a consideration of the differing market structures of these media. It is a follow-up to the suggestion by the appeals court in *C.C.C. v. Boulder* that the degree of natural monopoly (among other things) may make certain kinds of regulations constitutionally permissible in one medium that would be forbidden in another. The basis for variable balancing of individual and collective interests, then, becomes the degree to which a given medium is open to multiple voices. While the categories of media are nominal, the scale upon which judgments are based is continuous. The greater the accessibility to the medium for different viewpoints, the less the need for state intervention to encourage such diversity. Alternatively, the less the openness of the system, the greater the need for balancing in favor of the interests of the collective. In fact, up to the point of including cable, this analytic framework describes well the results, if not the rationale, of the court's consideration of the often conflicting rights of whole versus part. Speech and print are at the libertarian end of this spectrum, offering almost unlimited access to anyone who wishes to stand on a stump in a public park and yell, or to print up 100 political tracts and mail them to friends (or enemies). At the other recognized end is the natural scarcity of channels of broadcasting and the attendant First Amendment obligation of the broadcaster. Somewhere in the middle is cinema, with greater rights than the broadcaster but, still, apparently less than the street-corner orator.[7]

Use of an economic rationale for this First Amendment framework would, it seems, yield similar results. Broadcasting would still seem to be the most difficult forum to enter and speech the easiest. In addition, the failed market approach would provide some continuity for decision making, providing an underlying rationale common to all media yet still distinguishing among them. Further, and most important for present purposes, it would logically and easily fold in any new media that might develop, including cable television.

A special case in point might be the plethora of new forms of over-the-air broadcasting that are beginning to emerge in the marketplace. (Some popular new technologies, such as teletext and viewdata services, are not distribution services in this sense, but are forms of content and so not relevant to this scheme.) Low Power Television, Multi-Point Distribution Systems and even the long-awaited Direct Broadcast Satellite service are new technologies to some but, under this framework, merely variants of broadcasting; they do not constitute a new distribution system in this legal sense. What they do foretell is the possible widening of the broadcast marketplace. To the extent that they call into place new channels, they expand the potential for greater access and reduce the necessity of constitutional remedies to barriers to entry. This, of course, implies support for those who call for deregulation of broadcasting. And even the Supreme Court has noted the changing nature of this industry, a change in economics that could lead to a change in constitutional status.

Such changes must be restricted to broadcasting, however. They do not and cannot signal an expansion in the number or variety of cable outlets; cable represents a different form of communication system with a different economic structure.

Judicial acceptance of cable television's strong and acknowledged status as a natural economic monopoly would, therefore, put it at the far end of the closed market scale and provide firm ground for the invocation of social First Amendment interests and subsequent equitable balancing of the competing constitutional claims. It is the key to any First Amendment model of cable rights that seeks full protection for the legitimate First Amendment claims of society and its citizens.

It has been argued here, however, that similar proposals have fallen under the weight of *Tornillo*, that such market considerations have been rejected by the court as evidenced in that case. A closer examination reveals this not to be the case, however. The schema outlined above rests on the distinction between various media forms: broadcasting, print, cable. The decision in *Tornillo* did not hinge on such a broad analysis. The argument presented to the court there dealt specifically with newspapers. It moved from a position that concentration and monopoly in the daily newspaper industry warranted a reappraisal of First Amendment doctrine. The focus of subsequent analysis of the decision has been on the newspaper industry and its market structure, a structure arguably analogous to that of the cable industry. But herein lies the heart of the confusion, for the analogy is mistaken; it is inappropriate to draw a constitutional parallel between cable and newspapers. The appropriate analogy is between cable and print. With respect to *Tornillo*, it is important to keep in mind that newspapers are only a subclass of the print medium, and if the focus of that case can be shifted to consideration of the full range of print outlets, its ability to be generalized to other media is significantly diminished.

At the same time, this analytic framework need not change the outcome of *Tornillo* with respect to newspapers. In fact, if the court had followed strictly the criteria suggested above with respect to the openness of the market, it would have had to come to the same conclusion. Because the issue must be settled in terms of access to the medium, and because newspapers represent only a small portion of the available print media, there is little to justify access requirements. The collective has a nearly unlimited range of news and opinion in the print medium if it desires to seek it. Conversely, the same may not be said for cable. Cable is a medium unto itself and, unlike the print medium, not readily open to general and easy access by the individual without government intervention. Unlike print, control of that medium is singularly invested in any given area and a case similar to *Tornillo*, if based upon the equitable protection model, would come out much differently.

There is little to suggest that the Supreme Court had this framework in mind when it ruled in *Tornillo*. Nonetheless, were it to accept such an approach, the decision in that case would not have to be altered. Much of the language, in fact, could be used to support a broad failed market theory and could help to build an equitable protection model of First Amendment rights for cable. The two do not have to conflict.

The ability of the equitable protection model to satisfy competing claims is, therefore, clear. Further, its potential for being accepted by the courts as a viable solution to the cable dilemma already has been demonstrated in the decision by the U.S. District Court of Rhode Island in *Berkshire Cablevision v. Burke*.[8] There, the district court adopted the rationale behind the equitable protection model, citing inherent differences between cable and print, and finding that Rhode Island regulations requiring mandatory public access channels did not violate the First Amendment. In handing down the decision, the court, as previously noted, directly challenged the logic and dicta of the Eighth Circuit in *Midwest Video II*, where the appeals court found similar access rules to be an unconstitutional imposition on cablecasters.

Most of the court's justification came in cable's admitted natural monopoly, and the analysis here fell directly in line with that suggested by the equitable protection model. Specifically, the judge suggested that *Tornillo* was not applicable because it did not address a problem of monopoly in a medium of communication.

> Clearly, then, one of the basic issues in the instant case is whether or not economic "scarcity" is a constitutionally sufficient rationale for the regulation of cable television. While it is true that the Supreme Court has rejected economic scarcity as a basic for the regulation of newspapers, the lack of any access requirement for newspapers simply does not prevent a member of the general public from expressing his opinions in that same medium, which in such a case is print, of course.[9]

The court said that a citizen might then pamphleteer without great expense, but could not reasonably express his ideas through cable without the $7 million needed to build a system. And the court expressed confidence that such a distinction would not be ignored were the issue to come before the Supreme Court.[10] Concluded the judge, "scarcity is scarcity," and whether it comes in economic or physical form is irrelevant if its effect is to "remove from all but a small group an important means of expressing ideas."[11]

As the courts are increasingly presented with questions of cable's constitutional status, they may choose between the classic newspaper model suggested by the law as it stands, or they may shape new law, as they did in broadcasting, accepting for cable the truly special circumstance of market monopoly. And if the judiciary is then called upon to reconcile this new interpretation with *Tornillo,* the rationale outlined here will serve as well as any (and probably better than most) to lend coherence to First Amendment law in situations involving conflicting social and individual rights.

Parameters of the Equitable Protection Model

The failed market theory serves at the outset as the underpinning, the special circumstances, required for the use of countervailing social First Amendment interests. It is the hub of the equitable protection model which subsequently offers two important First Amendment benefits: first, a practical recognition of the restricted access to cable television as it is currently structured, and second, the philosophical recognition of a need to balance individual and social rights as a result of that restriction.

The logistics of that balancing remains a problem, however. The failed market theory has been used, at least in part, by other models, leading to numerous and varied controls on content, structure, and behavior. Simply proposing that conflicting rights be balanced, therefore, is insufficient. The limits of that balancing must be specified. Those limits are, in fact, suggested by the legal rationale itself. The aim, after all, is to supply the collective with as wide a variety of information and opinion as is available in the market-place. And it should be clearly understood that the role of the state is no more than to facilitate the availability of such views; it does not extend to the creation of diversity itself. That is, the state, acting for the collective, does not create new and different opinion for the sake of variety. Its only obligation is to remove barriers to such access that might arise via market or other forces. At the same time, the state has an obligation in the assertion of social interests to tread no more heavily on individual rights than is absolutely necessary in order to secure its purpose.

The legitimate claim of the collective, then, is that the full variety of viewpoints have access to the system, and the state's role, as representative of the collective, is to insure such access in the manner least offensive to the First Amendment rights of the system operator. The equitable protection model provides a relatively narrow corridor for state action: It is limited to maintaining access to the system. The model is, in short, a special form of access requirement grounded in First Amendment theory; it gives the people a constitutional right of access to cable while protecting the cable operator from most regulations by the state. This is distinguished from access requirements grounded in legislative or regulatory law with minimal regard for the interests of the cablecaster.

The mechanism by which access is insured is not as important as who retains control of the mechanism. Given the constitutional importance of the question and the necessity of balancing interests in a First Amendment context, the task of final oversight for application of the access standard must fall to the courts. The job of the courts has traditionally been to consider and act as arbiters in such matters. Trust has been placed in the courts to perform these functions, and they must do so in application of the equitable protection model with due regard for the sensitive rights of both sides.

Actual mechanisms for the control of access can be as simple as a court order on behalf of a citizen denied access to the cable system. No other government body need be involved since the claim is based on the First Amendment right of the collective to receive that opinion (coupled with the First Amendment right of the individual to speak, a factor that is not necessary for assertion of the right but helps reinforce it). On the other hand, local governmental bodies may wish to attempt the establishment of standards and processes by which system resources are made available for expressive activities, perhaps in concert with the industry. The model does not prohibit such guidelines or statutes as long as they meet with the approval of the courts as proper methods for the balancing of competing interests. Access requirements that impose too heavily on the cablecaster may, in the judgment of the court, be unconstitutional as violations of individual rights. Alternatively, nongovernmental spokesmen for the community may argue that the proposals are inadequate for the satisfaction of community needs. Again, the courts must strike the constitutional compromise, guided by the desire to see all sides, including that of the cable operator, afforded opportunity for expression.

In practice, therefore, the equitable protection model would not require a specified number of access channels, although such a requirement could be accommodated. Since access for individual expressions is the chief goal, such access could be provided through any number of systematic or nonsystematic methods. The cable company might voluntarily provide convenient times on one or more channels in response to specific access requests, or the courts in response to individual requests for access might intercede and require a half an hour of access at one time, an hour of access at another time. On the surface, this might seem an inefficient approach, but where requests for access are low, it would not overburden the courts, and alternatives that legislatively set aside channels that are never used would be the true inefficiencies.

Alternatively, this constitutionally based right of access cannot be seen as a wedge to force open an unlimited number of channels to every entrepreneur with an idea for a specialized channel; it is not a First Amendment substitute for leased access. In this context, access refers to and accommodates discrete messages—political, artistic, literary, scientific, and so forth. It is a means of opening the system to diverse expression for community benefit and is grounded in the collective's constitutional interest, not the individual's. Therefore, it is not a formula for opening a vein and securing full-channel commercial entry, but rather a narrow constitutional means of gaining access for specific messages or programs.

Once again, it does not forbid institutionalized access channels, but it does not require them either, and entry into the system can be as limited as that provided in case-by-case adjudication.

In return for the provision of this minimal access service, the cable company would be freed of virtually all other government controls. There would be, in the first instance, no possibility of municipal franchising—no licensing of communications systems. If a competing cable system or systems wished to vie for the attention and dollars of a city or suburb, that would be their right, the same right assured magazine and book publishers, shoe shops and fish merchants. This is unlikely to be the case, of course, but where the service of a monopoly company is uniformly bad, the temptation would be great for a potential competitor to step in and attempt to provide a lucrative, superior service. The threat of such intervention might be sufficient to spur improvement in the established system.

In any event, service and rates would be established by market mechanisms and not by the state or the city. The only possible state interference in rate setting might come through antitrust action. If a company could be shown to maintain market dominance through illegal anticompetitive practices, then action could be taken to restore the natural process of pricing and competition.

Other behavioral controls, such as community ascertainment would be equally forbidden, although a cable company would be subject to all normal business controls and taxes associated with other industries, the only fiat being that such controls not be aimed at manipulating content.

Structural controls also would fall under the weight of the First Amendment. The size of the cable system and the neighborhoods it served would not be a decision for a city council. If a given area could not be wired economically, the company would be under no legal obligation to wire it. Individuals in that area would have to demonstrate the economic feasibility of bringing in a system or system branch.

Neither could a city demand that a specified number of channels be established. If a company felt it could prosper by offering 40 instead of 120 channels, it would have the right to do so, although, in practice, companies competing for a new area would probably offer all the channels economically possible at the time, and the company that stayed with 12 channels when state-of-the-art systems provided 200 would be asking for competition.

Ownership of a system could not constitutionally be the subject of legislation, and if a company or individual desired to acquire multiple cable systems, a chain of systems, only the antitrust laws would stand as a barrier to unlimited development.

Finally, and most importantly, the municipality, the state and the federal government, would be forbidden from interfering with the content of cable television. All the constitutionally acceptable controls on expression—libel, privacy, obscenity, and so forth—would obviously be applicable to cable programming. But beyond these well-defined areas, the material distributed over the cable wires would be subject only to the editorial judgment of the system operator and access users. Viewer acceptance of certain programming would play a large role in the cable menu, but no city official would be permitted to ban a program or class of programs on grounds of moral objectionability or political disagreement.

Moreover, authorities would be prohibited from requiring the carriage of programming, be it city council meetings or the local broadcast station. "Must-carry" rules, in short, would be seen as in *Quincy* as violations of the cablecaster's rights. Again, it seems unlikely that cablecasters would black out major broadcast signals in the area, but to the extent that fringe signals or minor station signals were blacked out, those broadcasters could seek refuge in antitrust laws that forbid activities designed to drive them out of business. Given the monopoly market leverage of a cablecaster, such a case would seem to have some hope for success.

Generally, then, the equitable protection model seeks, through access, to provide an open forum for views and opinions from all social segments on the grounds of the social need for such interchange, but it seeks to do so without overly restricting the rights of the cable operator to program and conduct business at his or her discretion.

Summary

The question of the appropriate model of First Amendment rights for cable television is a current and important one. The courts today are grappling with the complex problems of how to fit cable into our modern constitutional framework. The dilemma isn't new and, in the course of cable's history, it has been approached in many ways. The Congress, the FCC and the courts have progressed through several stages of thinking about cable and the First Amendment, with the assumed nature of cable rights typically trailing a specific perceived definition of the technology and its role in society. The earliest perception of CATV as a passive conduit for television signals militated against substantial consideration of possible First Amendment rights, and a subsequent vision of cable as a facilitator of widespread community interaction and expression culminated in a notion of rights tilted toward a public utility model. For several years cable was seen as the utopian communication system, something to truly provide a twentieth century marketplace of ideas. Only with substantial changes in the political climate and increased outspokenness on the part of the industry did there develop a growing concern about potential First Amendment rights of the cable owner-operator, and a concomitant reevaluation of the logical foundation upon which those earlier conceptions of cable rights rested.

Today, there is a growing tendency to assume that cable should be left alone, that system programming is the sole purview of the cable owner, and that the owner has little or no social obligation. Access channels are seen as a burden on private interests. The problem, then, is how to reconcile two very contrasting positions of cable's social role.

This book has attempted to identify and analyze the fundamental philosophical barrier to fashioning a more appropriate model of cable rights, that being the problem of equitably balancing individual and collective First Amendment claims against the medium. It is suggested that the method of balancing these interests is grounded in the important underlying dimension of the inherent social utility in expression. As currently practiced, most models of First Amendment rights can find their place somewhere along a continuum of social utility, depending on the assumed goals of the given model. Therefore, various models of cable rights can be tested against this continuum. In doing so, however, the commonly used or proposed models of cable rights—print, broadcast, public forum, common carrier, and public utility—are found to be defective on either practical or philosophical grounds. That is, they either fail to balance individual and collective rights, or they lack a legitimate rationale for the invocation of collective First Amendment interests that is required before such balancing can take place. In the end, one can only conclude that under current constitutional interpretation, only the print model of cable rights is logically acceptable, and so nearly every form of federal, state, and local control over cable television violates the First Amendment rights of the cable operator.

But, since this conclusion does not satisfy the proposed aim of constitutional balancing—that is, the mutual satisfaction of collective as well as individual rights—a reinterpretation of the pivotal *Miami Herald v. Tornillo* case is required. Such a reinterpretation would leave intact the outcome of the case as it pertains to newspapers, but would eliminate the possibility of generalizing the case to cable. This would permit the adoption of equitable balancing on the legitimate basis of market monopoly in one specifically defined medium. The result would be a model of cable rights that served the valid claims of the collective while preventing unwarranted infringement of the rights of the cable operator.

The equitable protection model could help establish a means of realizing the long-sought promise of cable television's capacity to provide an electronic forum, both nationally and locally, for the expression of diverse and antagonistic views and, perhaps, serve to resolve some of the current legal problems that stand in the way of such a promise.

Throughout its history, cable has been the pawn of governments trying to open new avenues of communication to the public and, almost as often, trying to open new streams of revenue for municipal coffers. In the process, many of the potential constitutional rights of system operators have been trampled. Now, however, the pendulum is quickly swinging the other way. States and cities are losing control over what could be an important and legitimate First Amendment resource. While due respect for the rights of system operators is important, the obligation of monopoly communication services to the public is equally as critical. The door to public access is swinging closed. The logic of current constitutional law is catching up to cable regulation. Without a reinterpretation of the law as it applies to cable, the medium could become increasingly unresponsive to its social responsibility as a powerful and monopolistic information system to be open to political, cultural, and ideological diversity. This would be a tragic misuse of a great technology. With luck and foresight, however, the public, the industry, and the government will adopt a balanced approach to cable control. It is hoped that the discussion here will be of some small help in these deliberations.

Notes

1. *See e.g. City of Issaquah v. Teleprompter,* 611 P.2d 741 (1980).
2. *See e.g.,* Henderson, "Municipal Ownership of Cable Television: Some Issues and Problems," 3 *Comm/Ent* 667 (1981).
3. The traditional laws governing libel, privacy, obscenity, and so forth would, of course, also apply as they do for all media.
4. *See, e.g. F.C.C. v. Pacifica.*
5. *See, e.g. Red Lion.*
6. This can range from the corner pamphleteer to the U.S. Postal Service, but includes commercial merchandising and newspaper carriers.
7. *See e.g. Star v. Preller,* 419 U.S. 956 (1974) (upholding film licensing procedures that met with standards of due process).
8. *Berkshire Cablevision v. Burke,* 571 F. Supp. 976 (1983).
9. *Id.* at 986.
10. *Id.*
11. *Id.*

Index

About the Author

Patrick Robert Parsons received his Ph.D. in mass communication from the University of Minnesota in 1984. He currently is an assistant professor in the School of Communications at The Pennsylvania State University.